Parables of Jesus

Dr. Daniel Kazemian

New Harbor Press

RAPID CITY, SD

Kazemian/New Harbor Press
1601 Mt. Rushmore Rd, Ste 3288
Rapid City, SD 57701
www.newharborpress.com

Ordering Information:
Quantity sales. Special discounts are available on quantity purchases by corporations, associations, and others. For details, contact the "Special Sales Department" at the address above.

Parables of Jesus/Daniel Kazemian. -- 1st ed.
ISBN 978-1-63357-304-8

Contents

CHAPTER ONE

What is A Parable?

A typical story of a parable would have an earthly narrative with a heavenly meaning. A parable can create insight for anyone who is a believer or even though, for those who are not a follower of Christ. Some of the parables have a spiritual sense for every life. Jesus's tales will never disprove the Word of God. He always reached out to communicate easily with a simple story to open people's minds that they may experience the love of God.

What's the purpose of parables? The disciples of Jesus asked Him: tell us, what the use of your parables that you are teaching? Jesus answered: **"Therefore I speak to them in parables, because seeing they do not see, and hearing they**

do not hear, nor do they understand." Matthew 13:13, NKJV.

We will apply those parables in our lives because the living Word of God would change and transforming us. It can be a very beneficial source to a Christian church today. An illustration would be a great way to reach out for sharing the Gospel and especially using for outreach to non-believers in our new daily language and activities.

The Holy Spirit wants us to read a parable going deep into the Word of God and learning the message of God. We look at Jesus, how He made many excellent stories in different ways to communicate with His listeners. It made a positive parable with a simple word.

All Parables of Jesus from the Bible are straightforward, even though remarkably influential, fascinating, and essential, they can conform to our current ways of life into modern tales of Jesus. Parables of Jesus interpreted, it's interesting, relating to any seasons. It's exciting and is encouraging to read. It will be used for a practical purpose.

All stories of Jesus are compelling and are very dynamic. It's genuine of the Word of God. We believe the real purpose of Jesus' narratives for our good to lead us into the knowledge of God. It's necessary to meditate in the truth of the meaning of a story.

Jesus told most of His teaching and preaching with magnificent parables. As we know, Jesus tried to reach out to the people in a simple way. The people can understand a parable, an illustration, or a story presented to explain a message. Jesus needed to use often a short story and referred to the everyday society, rules, and conditions of life. He wanted to demonstrate the audiences to reveal God's power and authority to people in a simple manner they would have to learn.

I will be sharing from all great Jesus' stories, tales, His signs, wonders, healing, and His teaching from four books of the Gospels. Then we will be searching deep into all parables to learn why Jesus spoke such an easy way to teach us about the New Life in Him. In all four books in the New Testament would be a witness to perform the glory of Jesus.

CHAPTER TWO

Parables in
the Book of Matthew

Jesus Fulfills the Law: Jesus taught that He came not to abolish the Law or the Prophets, but he came to fulfill the Law. The Law of God will never change or will not pass away. The practice of Law is biblical law, commandments, traditions, sacrifices, and the regular rules of the Old Covenant were God's plan. The Law is God's rules to obey, regarding His righteousness, His divine. His guidelines for the spiritual nature of His people. He established in the first five books of the Bible "Torah," called the Pentateuch, means five scrolls.

The Law is the highest image of God's character because God reveals His richness, which is in Him. Then, since God is good, the Law is perfect.

"Do not think that I have come to abolish the Law or the Prophets; I have not come to abolish them but to fulfill them" Matthew 5:17-20, NKJV.

Be the Salt and the Light: Jesus made a great statement of being Salt and Light. Let's study with a short review of this verse. It talks about a believer in Christ that must be on fire for God, to become salt, means not to lose his faith or passion or love for God. If the salt will lose its flavor, and the salt cannot be used any longer. Saying to this: A believer must walk in purity and holiness to love Jesus with all his heart, soul, and mind. If the salt does not have a good flavor for using it for the right purpose, it will throw the salt away. If a believer does not keep his faith and not following Jesus, it can become a lukewarm Christian believer.

Another verse that Jesus mentioned here: A believer must live in the light, He said, I am the Light of the world. Jesus said: a city is on the uphill is needed to have a light to be seen by everyone, and it cannot be hidden. He said: A lamp makes a light, and it cannot put it under a basket but put it on a lampstand. The light gives shine to all around the house.

Be the light; He is the Light; we are in Jesus. Therefore, we are in the Light of the Lord Jesus. We shine before every man; then, they will recognize that we are in Christ. May others see the Light of Jesus in us; it will bring glory to the Father in Heaven.

"Let your light so shine before men, that they may see your good works and glorify your Father in heaven." Matthew 5:13-15, NKJV.

Murder Starts in the Heart: Here in this story reveals to us that a murder will occur in the heart. Jesus said: you have heard in the past, do not murder. You will be judged according to your heart. If you are offering your gift onto the Lord and do not do it, leave it there on the Alter. If you have anything against your brother or your brother had something against you. You need to reconcile with your brother, then come back to the Alter to offer your gift to the Lord.

You need to make peace and having forgiveness with your brother. God is the judge who is watching over your life, and your adversity is putting you in judgment. Let your affliction pay less for your sins, hand over to God. Jesus said: Reconcile with your God that you will not pay more penalty of your sins, then come back to worship God through your offering.

"Therefore, if you bring your gift to the altar, and there remember that your brother has something against you, leave your gift there before the altar, and go your way. First, be reconciled to your brother, and then come and offer your gift." Matthew 5:21-26, NKJV.

Serving Others to Please God: Jesus shared when we will have the heart to help others by doing a good a charitable deed, not to be seen by any man. God sees our hearts, and He has a great reward stored for us. When we try to serve someone who needs help. Jesus said, do not be a hypocrite and not making any sound of a trumpet in the synagogues or the streets. Do not have any glory for yourselves. No one will give you any glory or rewarding you by your acts of serving.

A prideful man will block the reward of God for himself. Pride of man removes God's blessings. When we do serving and a charitable deed for others, we do it in the secret place. God sees our hearts, and if we serve others in the name of

Jesus. He will receive all the honor and glory for Himself.

When we serve the people, we will keep silent, not even let your left hand know what your right hand is doing. Jesus wants us to minister to others for the Glory of His name. He is rewarding us to every work we do for His people.

"that your charitable deed may be in secret; and your Father who sees in secret will Himself reward you openly." Matthew 6:1-4, NKJV.

Prayer to the Father: Jesus began to teach about prayer, and this is the familiar teaching of Jesus. He taught us how to come into worship and to seek God's presence. Do not be like others would like to be hypocrites. They would like to pray in the synagogues and standing on the corners of the street that other people will see them. Anyone who will pray, go to your room, not to be seen by any man.

God will see your heart, and He sees you in your secret place that you are seeking Him. He will reward you openly. Do not waste your time as the heathen will be doing. Because they want to pray aloud and to pray with many words, it will not get any reward from Heavenly Father. He said, when you pray, ask your Father, He knows what you need. Therefore, you pray like this:

Our Father in heaven,
Hallowed be Your name.
Your kingdom come.
Your will be done
On earth as it is in heaven.
Give us this day our daily bread.
And forgive us our debts,
As we forgive our debtors.
And do not lead us into temptation,
But deliver us from the evil one.
For Yours is the kingdom and the power and the glory forever. Amen.

Jesus encouraged us to forgive others, which our Father will forgive our sins. If we do not forgive others, those who have hurt us in the past, it will bring hinders in getting our prayers answered from the Father. Sometime, our early life will bring back past experience. And the Lord will show us we must forgive others. If we cannot forgive other people, how can we expect that God will forgive our sins as well? Let's ask Him to give us His grace to have the power to forgive others. We need to walk in His kindness to become a loving person toward others. Matthew 6:5-15, NKJV.

Fasting for God, Not for Man: Jesus describes here about Fasting, and the Lord will teach us not to be hypocrites. He encourages us to take Fasting for the Lord with a happy face, not a sad face. Jesus said: Is anyone who will fast, anoint your head, and clean your face that no one can recognize you are fasting. God will reward you in the secret place of your fasting openly. Fasting and seeking God can encourage us to build up our knowledge over our spiritual dreams and daily ministry. There will be a purpose of fasting to get the focus off of ourselves than anything else but the Lord.

There is a plan of God for all of us to fast and to seek God for directions and guidance. Fasting is leading us to a new plan of God, and then we will do the will of God humbly. Fasting is essential for the Christian faith believers who are experiencing in the spirit of victory in Christ.

"so that you do not appear to men to be fasting, but to your Father who is in the secret place; and your Father who sees in secret will reward you openly." Matthew 6:16-18, NKJV.

Store Up Treasures in Heaven:

We must cherish the Lord with His goodness; Jesus is our great treasure. Jesus is talking about treasure here; how can we get a spiritual treasure from Him? Earthly treasure can be like: Money, wealth, gold, cash, jewel, valuable things, property, etc.

The Lord will reveal to us through His Words, saying, if we keep our treasure on earth, where our hearts will also be. It will die out every wealth in this world and disappeared in a matter of time. If we continue our faith in the Word and stay firm to trust in the Lord Jesus. He will never leave or forsake us. We can have eternal life, and it is our treasures in heaven. We will give our ability, our wealth, our way of life, our ministry to the work of the Kingdom.

"Do not lay up for yourselves treasures on earth, where moth and rust destroy and where thieves break in and steal; but lay up for yourselves treasures in heaven, where neither moth nor rust destroys and where thieves do not break in and steal. For where your treasure is, there your heart will be also." Matthew 6:19-21, NKJV.

The Lamp of the Body: The Lord Jesus is describing that the lamp is the eye of the human body. I think it symbolizes the lamp is a source of spiritual eyes. If the body cannot have a good eye, it will not see the light, and the body goes into darkness. The good eyes as a lamp making light. If the lamp is operating in good condition can give guidance of souls and body. The Lord Jesus will bring the Light into our sinful world, and He is the Light of the world. He is the One can come into our spiritual darkness, making Light into the darkness of our souls and bodies.

As we experience, he came by God the Father's plan into the dark world. The Father loves the whole world that He gave His only begotten Son, to die on the cross for all humanity to bring them back to arms of the loving Father.

If we accept Him by faith and recognize Him as the Son of God. By faith, we can have the love and forgiveness of Jesus and receiving His peace, His joy in the Holy Spirit. Believe in Jesus. He is the only Savior to bring us into salvation and Eternal life. We become light in the darkness. Amen.

"The lamp of the body is the eye. If therefore your eye is good, your whole body will be full of light. But if your eye is bad, your whole

body will be full of darkness. If therefore the light that is in you is darkness, how great is that darkness!" Matthew 6:22-23, NKJV.

Cannot Serve God and Riches: We learn from Jesus to encourage us to worship God in the spirit and truth. In this teaching, Jesus shared that no one can serve God and mammon. It means we cannot worship God or love God and, at the same time, we follow other gods. We cannot continue to serve two masters. Jesus said: you must love God from all your heart, your souls, and your mind.

The other one will represent the mammon wealth or love money referred to as an evil ambition of worship. We follow the Lord Jesus, to become loyal to the One who is worthy in all praise. We must serve God and not serve the mammon.

"No one can serve two masters; for either he will hate the one and love the other, or else he will be loyal to the one and despise the other. You cannot serve God and mammon." Matthew 6:24, NKJV.

Do Not Worry: This is a powerful word of inspiration from the Lord, not to worry about anything. Jesus encouraged us, do not worry about your life: what to eat or what to drink. Not worry about your body what to wear or what putting on your body. What is important about being worried? Is it food or clothing? Jesus said: if you look at the birds of the air, they don't sow or reap even they don't store up in the barn. Your Heavenly Father will feed them. How valuable are you in the eyes of God more than anything else that He will take care of you? Can worry add one day in your life?

The Lord Jesus is sharing not to worry about our future life. See the lilies of the field, and we don't know how they grow, how the root with soil started to develop to get flourished. Even Jesus said, King Solomon, with all his glory and all his riches, was not dressed up beautifully like one of these. Look at the grass of the fields; the Lord will take care of nature for today and tomorrow. He is our provider. How precious we are in the eyes of God that He will be looking after us.

Therefore, Jesus said, do not worry about today, nor tomorrow. Let your Father in heaven will guide your life daily if we believe in Him. We have strong faith and trust in His Words, asking Him to give us confidence in the Holy Spirit. Our hearts will tell us that we are secure in His mighty Hands of God. The Lord said: Your Father knows about your needs.

Seek the Kingdom of God with all your heart, with all your might first. Then other things in life will be added unto you. Being worry is not helping us. Jesus said, let the worry of the day or tomorrow will do about its own things. We live one day at the time, living with God day by day. He is controlling our daily life. Rejoice in His presence. He is Good, and He is faithful.

"Therefore do not worry, saying, 'What shall we eat?' or 'What shall we drink?' or 'What shall we wear?' For after all these things the Gentiles seek. For your heavenly Father knows that you need all these things. But seek first the kingdom of God and His righteousness, and all these things shall be added to you. Therefore do not worry about tomorrow, for tomorrow will worry about its own things. Sufficient for the day is its own trouble." Matthew 6:25-34, NKJV.

Not Judge Others: The Lord is speaking about; do not judge, not making a judgment of people. If we condemn or judge someone, Jesus said: you shall be judged according to your words and deeds. Every word we use to make others uncomfortable, and it will come back to us as the same words we used for them. He mentioned: Why do we look at the speck in our brother's eyes, but not looking at our own eyes.

Usually, we cannot see the plank in our own eyes. We will say to our brother, let me help you to take the speck out of your eyes. That's why Jesus said: You are a hypocrite!

First, if we look at our eyes and check our hearts, we will cleanse ourselves and coming into God's presence. If we are not in Christ, and God will remove all our unrighteousness out of our lives. We see ourselves clearly who we are in the Lord, and Jesus accepts us and forgives us. We are honoring Him with our lives.

"You hypocrite, first take the plank out of your own eye, and then you will see clearly to remove the speck from your brother's eye." Matthew 7:1-5, NKJV.

Asking, Seeking, and Knocking: Jesus is encouraging us in this verse; Asking, it shall be given to you. Seeking, you will find it. Knocking, it shall be open to you. These words are a powerful promise of God for all of us. When we search for Him, the Lord will draw near to us, and He manifests His promises to us. There is a reward for those who 'Ask,' 'Seek,' 'knock.'

Another parable Jesus mentioned here that if your son asks for bread, do you give him a stone? If your son will ask for a fish, do you give him a serpent? Jesus said that the evil person does not know how to give gifts to his children.

How much your Father in Heaven who loves to give good gifts to those who ask Him. Continue to search for Him and knocking on the door of His blessing. He will pour out His blessings on you.

"Ask, and it will be given to you; seek, and you will find; knock, and it will be opened to you." Matthew 7:7-12, NKJV.

The Narrow Way: Jesus will show us in this verse about the narrow gate. It's called the narrow door to life. Jesus predicted; which road we choose, the "narrow gate" to eternal life and the "broad road," which brings us to destruction. It sets forth that many souls will stand between on two roads; the road of new Life or the road to hell 'destruction.' But Jesus mentioned that false teachers would try to make human laws and procedures, wrong religion, or spiritual man-rules.

Jesus responds that narrow is the door and narrow the pathway brings to life, and simply a few could receive it. We need to recognize that "Jesus is the door" only, which we all must enter through Him to receive eternal life. Jesus said: *I am the Way, the Truth, and the Life.* John 14:6, NKJV. We cannot find any other way because He is the only door to a new life. Many will seek God in another direction to find the truth. They will struggle to go through difficulty in life.

These people will accept the broad road that leads to everlasting destruction. As we are born-again Christian, we can hear Jesus' voice and follow Him, where He is leading us to eternal life. If we decide to enter the narrow gate, we make the right choice. No one will usually obtain heaven by doing good in life; we receive it by faith.

In fact, many people in other religions will seek and trying to enter the Kingdom of God. But it is difficult because of the life of a mortal pride, living in sins, all of these things which take place against us in receiving eternal life. Jesus is our Grace, and we receive Him by faith. We invite Him in our hearts as Lord and Savior.

"Enter by the narrow gate; for wide is the gate and broad is the way that leads to destruction, and there are many who go in by it.

Because narrow is the gate and difficult is the way which leads to life, and there are few who find it." Matthew 7:13-14, NKJV.

Recognize Them by Their Fruits: When we experience in our ways of life, every activity and every action will come out of our hearts. If the heart is pure in God's sight, it will bring spiritual fruits. Because God has given us a free choice, we make our own decision in life. Some sins can grow in our hearts, just like every sin would produce bad fruit and will give us a terrible harvest. It can build up from a sinful heart. The work of evil spirits bears poor fruit.

Jesus said; there is a good tree that produces good fruit, but the bad tree produces bad fruit. A fruitful tree cannot bear bad fruit and a bad tree, it cannot also bear good fruit. Every tree will not produce good fruit; it would need to cut down and put them into the fire. So, therefore, you will recognize them by their fruits.

When Jesus replied, "You will know them by their fruit" dealing with false or deceitful teachers, He would give us spiritual understanding to discern them. Fake prophets or false speakers promote wrong messages. We need to understand their religious doctrine, and it would make it possible with their wrong teaching transferred to us. We don't have to be agreed with their thought. By the leadership of the Holy Spirit, He will guide us to discern their false messages carefully to see the fruits of their lives and ministry.

"A good tree cannot bear bad fruit, nor can a bad tree bear good fruit. Every tree that does not bear good fruit is cut down and thrown into the fire. Therefore by their fruits you will know them." Matthew 7:15-20, NKJV.

I Never Knew You: When Jesus answered, "I never knew you," said to the pretended or insincere followers. He referred to that He never identified them as His faithful disciples or His believers. Some will not be interested to hear anything about God, nor willing to accept the truth. They will not make any relationships with the Lord. Some will not allow Jesus to dwell in their hearts; even some will not take Him in their lives. Some would love to have the Word of Jesus in their lips. Therefore, many would like to preach the Word of God, but it doesn't mean anything to them, and it will not an impact on their personal life.

Jesus said many would come to Me, saying in that day:

Lord, **"have we not prophesied in Your name"** Matthew 7:22

Lord, **"cast out demons in Your name"** Matthew 7:22

Lord, **"done many wonders in Your name?"** Matthew 7:22

Jesus would say, I never recognized you. We go through the trial of life, and then we grow in a cold relationship with our Lord. Remark that Jesus is not separating us from His intimacy and with His followers here. When anyone who is making a commitment to Jesus and having a personal relationship with Him. We will see our spiritual fruits and how we are living in the Christian life with Him.

We will invite Jesus into our hearts, and He is the Lord of our lives. We have to choose to follow Him.

"And then I will declare to them, I never knew you; depart from Me, you who practice lawlessness!" Matthew 7:21-23, NKJV.

Wise and Foolish Builders: Jesus presented a powerful word to build our lives on the rock. He said: you hear my Word, obey it, and follow my plans, you will be wise. It's always a blessing to get a new revelation of the Holy Spirit to make the right decision. In this message, He said: if a wise man hears My Word, to have an obedient heart, then you build your house on the rock. If a foolish man makes his house on the sand, by storm and winds will be demolished, and it cannot stand.

When we are experiencing in the world, we deal with all the challenges of life daily. If we are building our faith in our ability can never stand, we will all fail soon. Jesus is the Rock, and He is a strong foundation of New Life. We recognize ourselves to believe in Him, and He will never fail us by any means in any crisis or problems of life. When the enemy attacks us, He will establish us by His Words to have a breakthrough to victory.

"But everyone who hears these sayings of Mine, and does not do them, will be like a foolish man who built his house on the sand: and the rain descended, the floods came, and the winds blew and beat on that house, and it fell. And great was its fall." Matthew 7:24-27, NKJV.

A Cost of Following Jesus: There was a certain scribe man came to Jesus, said: **"Teacher, I will follow You wherever You go."** Matthew 8:19, NKJV.

As we know, following Jesus can have a great dedication and having a submission under Jesus' authority to carry His cross daily. Also, are we willing to testify His name? He makes us filled with courage and boldness, not to be ashamed of His name? When we leave everything behind in this world to follow Jesus, we need to realize; there is a cost of discipleship to follow Him for the rest of our lives. We cannot leave Him a halfway. We believe in Him by faith, and we will finish our course until He comes back soon for His Church.

We are giving Jesus our commitments to all things first. Following Jesus is a beautiful experience. But Jesus responded to anyone who has left home, relatives, parents, children for the sake of my name will be rewarded in this life and receive eternal life. We always desire to love Him, and there is a cost to follow Jesus. And there will be a cost of serving Jesus because our mortal character becomes weak, not willing to go after the Lord. It will be hard to find new truth and having peace with God in the confusing world.

Today many people are searching for God, looking for the truth of life, but some people will go in the wrong way. The Word said; there is no other name that given to us under heaven that we shall be saved; it is the name of Jesus only. God has created us for a purpose to worship and serve Him more than anything else.

Nothing can satisfy us with temporary pleasure in this world, and everything will fade away with material things around us. We cannot love the world because there is nothing that can be found. Everything will be enjoyable for a short time. But living in the plan of God will satisfy us in life.

"Then another of His disciples said to Him, "Lord, let me first go and bury my father. But Jesus said to him, "Follow Me, and let the dead bury their own dead." Matthew 8:18-22, NKJV.

Jesus Called Matthew the Tax Collector: When Jesus passed and walked from there, He saw a man who was a Tax collector. In the time of Jesus's ministry, there was no one in society could love a tax collector because they were unfair and unjust to everybody in their days. There was a man named; Matthew, who was sitting in his office. Jesus saw him, said, "Follow Me." He heard that Jesus called him.

He suddenly came to himself, why Jesus called me into Himself. He thought it might be a plan of God upon me when Jesus saw me. But

Jesus saw Matthew and recognizes him that he is the chosen one who becomes a servant of God. Matthew left everything; he stood up, gave up his business; he followed Jesus.

Jesus entered a house, sitting around tables and having meals with every tax collector with all of His disciples. And those Pharisees saw the events, they didn't ask directly from Jesus, but they asked His disciples; why your Teacher sitting and having meals with all sinners and tax collectors?

At the same time, Jesus heard, He answered them: those people do not need any help. But these sinners and tax collectors need forgiveness of their sins. I came to crucify my life for all sinners of the world, and I brought grace and mercy from heaven for them.

Jesus said, the Father has not sent me to call the righteous man, but to call all sinners to repentance. When we recognize our sins, He is ready to come into our hearts to forgive all our sins.

"When Jesus heard that, He said to them, "Those who are well have no need of a physician, but those who are sick. But go and learn what this means: 'I desire mercy and not sacrifice.' For I did not come to call the righteous,

but sinners, to repentance." Matthew 9:9-13, NKJV.

Questioned About Fasting: Then, the disciples of John came to Jesus, and they were very curious about Fasting. They asked Jesus why we will Fast along with Pharisees as they taught us to do so, but why your disciples will not Fast? Jesus answered their questions: when the bridegroom is still here, they will not mourn as long as their bridegroom with them. When the time comes, and the Son of God will be taken away from them, they will do the Fasting.

Jesus is saying here: Fasting is essential for a Christian believer to seek God for having a breakthrough in Spiritual warfare. This verse is really encouraging for all Christians to Fast. In fact, fasting can be very healthy for our bodies. Fasting brings us closer to God and to make us humble to commit ourselves to His Words. Fasting will remove all unanswered prayer shall come to answer.

I have personally Fasted many days and weeks seeking God for a fresh spirit, and anointing of God came on me. He answered my prayer through Fasting. I encourage you to fast; I wrote about Fasting in my first book, "Manifestation of

Prayer." You may get one and to read one chapter about Fasting.

"Then the disciples of John came to Him, saying, "Why do we and the Pharisees fast often, but Your disciples do not fast?" And Jesus said to them, "Can the friends of the bridegroom mourn as long as the bridegroom is with them? But the days will come when the bridegroom will be taken away from them, and then they will fast." Matthew 9:14-15, NKJV.

New Cloth and Old Garment: There is a parable Jesus mentioned here: Do not patch a piece of cloth on an old garment. The patch will not be active with a new garment even become worse, and creating a big hole later on. It will not be used as a last long garment. Jesus said another word with other examples; do not take a new wine to pour in into old wineskins to blend. It breaks the skin, and suddenly the wineskins will be ruined. If we pour in a new wine into new wineskins, it will be preserved both together.

The meaning of the parable is: Jesus gave this illustration about if we accept a new life in the Lord, and it will be as our unique garment. If we try to make a patch in our old life, it will not be helpful. We need to leave the old life behind.

When we walk with a new life in Christ, we will accept a pure life in full, if we bring our past experience back to mix with a new life in Christ. It will not bear great fruit in spiritual growth.

Jesus also said about pouring in a fresh wine with new wineskins will be preserved. Do not live in the past; we live with a great future in life ahead of us and living with a new life in Christ. He will take us to a new way and a new truth and a new life with peace and joy and good health.

"Nor do they put new wine into old wineskins, or else the wineskins break, the wine is spilled, and the wineskins are ruined. But they put new wine into new wineskins, and both are preserved." Matthew 9:16-17, NKJV.

The Harvest Plentiful: After Jesus went to cities and villages to teach and to preach the Good News of the Kingdom of God. The compassion of Jesus was excellent, and He healed every sickness among the people. He saw the multitudes of people who were lost; they had no shepherd looking after them. He looked at the many people are depressed and scattered around, no directions of life, and not having the truth of God. And these people were like sheep.

His heart moved with great compassion said to His disciples: The harvest is plentiful, but the laborers are few. He said, pray to the Lord of the harvest to send more workers to go out to preach the Gospel into His harvest fields. It is true; we need more passionate believers to reach out to lost souls. How can we expect they will come into the salvation of the Lord without hearing the Good News of Jesus? There are many lost people are living without knowing the truth of God and not having experience with God's love.

When we ask God to prepare us and to lead us to the places which are needed, we become witnesses of Jesus. The passion of Jesus is to save lost souls, and they will receive the love of God and eternal life in the Lord Jesus.

"Then he said to his disciples, the harvest is plentiful but the workers are few. Ask the Lord of the harvest, therefore, to send out workers into his harvest field." Matthew 9:37-38, NKJV.

Having A Fear of God: Jesus taught His word about not having any fear of man. He encouraged every believer to hear the Word of truth and speaking boldly to the public. If they are trying to take away your faith and your words out of your heart, do not be afraid of any man's intimidation. Jesus said: you shall be witnesses of me. If they are trying to harm you because of me, they want to kill your body, but they cannot destroy your souls.

God is able to save many lives. He said, **"But rather fear Him who is able to destroy both soul and body in hell."** Matthew 10:28, NKJV. No one can come near to you or hurt you, because God is protecting His children from harm's way. Jesus gave a good illustration about He knows numbers of hairs of our head. He knows how He can take care of His children; we belong to Him, those whom they have chosen by Him.

The Lord is teaching us in this verse about the fear of God is reverence. It will be very extraordinary for us to respect the God of Israel. It must praise comes of the heart and to serve the Lord Jesus. The believer's fear is becoming an adoration and gratitude to God. We need genuinely to understand this admiration for every Christian can be godly fear.

The inspiring Word of God is a principle of God's Spirit and His presence for us to yield ourselves under God's authority. Remain firm in Him and having trust in His Name. He is our advocate; He is a strong Tower. He does beautiful wonders.

The fear of God is essential to our faith and believing in His ways. In fact, He served us by giving His life on the cross. He is serving and loving us every day. Biblical teaching about the fear of God for the Christian believer, we need to recognize that God hates sin. We all expect His judgment on sin. As a Born-again Christian, we are under His Grace; we are secure in His Hands.

Believers in Christ will not be intimidated by God, He is the Love, and He loves us. We don't need to be afraid of Him, His word and His mercy will accept us to be with Him. Nothing in the world can separate us from His Grace. His goodness will never give up on us. His Love will never forsake us. The concept of fearing of God is really getting such adoration for Him that it involves a high spiritual impact on our lives.

"Are not two sparrows sold for a copper coin? And not one of them falls to the ground apart from your Father's will. But the very hairs of your head are all numbered. Do not fear therefore; you are of more value than many sparrows." Matthew 10:27-31, NKJV.

Confess Jesus Before Men: As Christian believers, we still need to make another 'confession,' not only to do the repentance of sins, but we must confess Jesus as Lord and Savior. It is important to recognize Jesus before men, how we have received the forgiveness of our sins.

He commanded us to testify of His Good News. A Christian believer must speak the name of Jesus boldly and confess before any man without fear that Jesus is his Savior. When we recognize our sin and confess with our mouth that Jesus is Lord. Believing in our hearts, accepting Him as Lord and Savior, that God has raised Him from the dead. We receive the salvation of the Lord.

He declares that if we confess Him before men, He will acknowledge us before His Father in heaven. To accept Jesus is to demonstrate the message of God's love for humanity. It's the evidence that Jesus is our redemption, and He brought salvation to the entire world. If you are ready to receive Jesus and making your mind for having a spiritual experience with the Holy Spirit.

He is there, standing and knocking at the door of your heart. Jesus tells us now; let me come in. He loves to start a new walk of peace, joy with us. It means that we obey what the Word says, we would act on it by faith what He promised to make a change in our lives.

We shall acknowledge Him and preaching His powerful Word to all men. We continue serving Him; we will praise Him with our attitude and with our Christian lifestyle. We magnify Jesus, and we shall glorify the Father.

"Therefore whoever confesses Me before men, him I will also confess before My Father who is in heaven. But whoever denies Me before men, him I will also deny before My Father who is in heaven. " Matthew 10:32-33, NKJV.

Jesus Brings Division: In these phrases, Jesus says: As we know, the sword is the Word of God and is for righteousness and redemption. The sword cuts down into the deep core of man's mortal mind and man's spirit. Because of man's carnal mindset will still carry out with deception, wrongdoing, and with all evil actions. Thus, the sword reveals the truth of Jesus. The authoritative Word is penetrating and piercing the heart. The purpose of the sword "The Word" is powerful to change and to transform lives for the Glory of God.

Jesus spoke, He had appeared to the world, not to bring peace into the earth, but a sword which separates families. We see someone in the family will get saved and receiving the Lord Jesus to become a Christian believer. Then other members of the family are not having faith in Christ. It's bringing a hard time against the one who has received Jesus and living for Christ. It would set up some children against parents because of the faith in the Lord. It might be for those believers who are living in a different faith-based religion within their home.

When Jesus tells us, whoever giving up his life for my sake will find a new life. He reveals about believing in Him rather than serving other things in our own ambitions. If any man who becomes a child of God, and he would have to deny himself. When we are ready to pick up his cross daily, He gives us the strength to become comfortable in daily life. He will empower our faith to follow Him for the rest of our lives. He mentioned, He who gives up his life for my sake, he shall find it.

"And he who does not take his cross and follow after Me is not worthy of Me. He who finds his life will lose it, and he who loses his life for My sake will find it." Matthew 10:34-39, NKJV.

Serving and Receiving Reward: Many scriptures are talking about that God is the God of reward. It means, if we do good to others, He is the One who can bless us with a double-portion blessing. Jesus said he who will receive you in My name, will accept Me, He who sent Me. If there is a prophet among you, who serves you when you receive the prophet in the name of the prophet, you will receive the prophet's reward.

If there is a righteous man who would come among you and ready to serve you. Anyone who receives him in the name of a righteous man will receive his reward. Jesus mentioned here again, if anyone who is serving a little one who needs a cold cup of water in the name of my disciple, he will get his rewards greatly. He shall not lose his blessings.

In these phrases, Jesus is the servant, and He wants us to serve anyone who loves to minister as Jesus did. Serving shall be a passion for every Christian believer who loves God and to serve from the whole heart. We are as a Christian believer will be ready to minister someone who needs spiritual help.

"He who receives you receives Me, and he who receives Me receives Him who sent Me. He who receives a prophet in the name of a prophet shall receive a prophet's reward. And he who receives a righteous man in the name of a righteous man shall receive a righteous man's reward. And whoever gives one of these little

ones only a cup of cold water in the name of a disciple, assuredly, I say to you, he shall by no means lose his reward." Matthew 10:40-42, NKJV.

Rest in the Lord: Jesus was speaking to His Father in Heaven, said, Father, I thank you that you are the Lord of heaven and earth. You have covered these matters from the wise and thoughtful man and have acknowledged them to your children. He said no one would know the Son except the Father; at the same no one will know the Father except the Son. Jesus asked His Father to reveal everything to those chosen one who can believe the Son.

He encouraged us when we are weary and depressed in life. He will give us rest and peace. He will release His Spirit upon us. He carries us into His peace in the Holy Spirit, and we rest in His presence. He is compassionate and gracious in spirit, and you will find rest for your souls.

"Come to me, all you who are weary and burdened, and I will give you rest. Take my yoke upon you and learn from me, for I am gentle and humble in heart, and you will find rest for your souls. For my yoke is easy and my burden is light." Matthew 11:28-30, NKJV.

Jesus Is Lord of the Sabbath: As we believe, the Trinity is; God the Father as the Creator. God the Son as the Savior. God the Holy Spirit as the Teacher, Guider, Comforter. Three persons are One God. He is only the One who rules over the laws and authority that control the Sabbath day. Jesus is the Lord of the Sabbath. He had permission from the Father to override the Pharisees' practices and procedures because He had made the Sabbat.

God the Father, the Creator, is always higher than the creation of the world. Jesus challenged the lawmakers justly to describe the significance of the Sabbath and all the requirements relating to it. Because He is Lord of the Sabbath, Jesus is able to do whatever He wishes.

As Jesus had the absolute authority to discharge any rule or any tradition He wanted. That's why Jesus said: I am the Lord of the Sabbath had arrived. We believe by His death and resurrection, and He fulfilled the "Sabbath rest." So, we rest in His presence, we trust in His mighty Words. He is our Salvation and Redeemer of our sins.

"But if you had known what this means, 'I desire mercy and not sacrifice,' you would not have condemned the guiltless. For the Son of

Man is Lord even of the Sabbath." Matthew 12:1-8, NKJV.

Every Kingdom Divided Cannot Stand: They brought a Demon-possessed to Jesus, He cast them out all evil spirits from the man. He was also blind and mute; the Lord healed him. The leaders of Pharisees heard that Jesus cast out the demon out of the people, came and said: Is He casting out the demon by Beelzebub, the prince of demons. Jesus knew what they thought: He said: If every kingdom will divide against itself. Every house and every city will divide against itself; it cannot stand.

If Satan will cast out Satan, he will divide against himself, and it cannot stand also. How can his kingdom will stand? Then if I cast out a demon out of people, I do with the spirit of God, the Kingdom of God is near, and the Spirit is of God has come upon you.

"But if I cast out demons by the Spirit of God, surely the kingdom of God has come upon you." Matthew 12:24-28, NKJV.

The Unpardonable Sin: The Word said; if we do the blasphemy against the Holy Spirit, it cannot be forgiven. The Holy Spirit is here in our midst, and when the Lord Jesus ascended to heaven. He sat at the right hand of the Father. Jesus is not on earth, but the Father has sent the Holy Spirit to the earth and His church. There will not be possible anyone can see Jesus directly in our physical eyes.

But when the Holy Spirit came down to earth to help us and to reveal Jesus to us. He loves to open our spiritual eyes to see Jesus better. The Holy Spirit operates a miracle, and thus, He connects us to the spirit of truth. Jesus said, If someone continues to blaspheme against the Lord Jesus, He will forgive him. There will be no forgiveness for anyone who blasphemes against the Holy Spirit, and not in this age and nor the age to come.

"Therefore I say to you, every sin and blasphemy will be forgiven men, but the blasphemy against the Spirit will not be forgiven men. Anyone who speaks a word against the Son of Man, it will be forgiven him; but whoever speaks against the Holy Spirit, it will not be forgiven him, either in this age or in the age to come." Matthew 12:31-32, NKJV.

A Man Known by His Fruit: There is a powerful illustration that Jesus taught about a tree that gives good or bad fruit. Jesus mentioned here: if a tree is bad, it brings a bad fruit. He said: which one is bad: a tree is bad, or the fruit is bad. Then we recognize a tree from its own fruit. He goes on to teach about the heart of man is evil; every word speaks, is coming out of the heart. If a person is speaking good, is coming out of his heart. So, the heart is kind, gracious, out of man's heart, the mouth speaks sweet words.

How can a man be being evil in the heart and speak good things? Nothing good is coming out the month of any man who is living with an evil spirit and mind. Jesus said: If any man speaks any word out of his month is accountable for his action will give an account of the day of judgment. Your own words will justify you, and you will be condemned.

"Either make the tree good and its fruit good, or else make the tree bad and its fruit bad; for a tree is known by its fruit." Matthew 12:33-37, NKJV.

Pharisees Ask for a Sign: These Scribes and Pharisees asked Jesus for a sign. He said a corrupt generation seeks for a sign. There will be no sign that be given, except the manifestation of the sign of prophet Jonah. As we know, Jonah was inside a big fish for three days and three nights. Jesus said the Son of Man would also be there three days and three nights in the heart of the earth.

The people of Nineveh have repented by the preaching of Jonah, but this wicked generation will not repent their sins. Jesus said the Son of Man the higher than Jonah, who is here to declare the Kingdom of God. He mentioned that the Queen of the south would rise up with the people in judgment and condemn it. She appeared to discover the wisdom of Solomon. Indeed, Jesus is the higher than Solomon is to proclaim the Good News.

"The queen of the South will rise up in the judgment with this generation and condemn it, for she came from the ends of the earth to hear the wisdom of Solomon; and indeed a greater than Solomon is here." Matthew 12:38-42, NKJV.

An Unclean Spirit Returns: Jesus shared another illustration of the unclean spirit. When a man has an unclean spirit will leave from the man's life. The unclean spirit will go out to find a dry place to rest, but will not find any dwelling. The house got cleaned after the unclean spirit left the house. The unclean spirit will say to himself, and I will go back to where I came from? The unclean spirit will bring back seven more evil spirits; they dwell in it and entering into the clean house.

Jesus said: The house represents our heart and our spirit. If we allow the evil spirit will come back into a clean heart and a pure soul and a clear mind. The devil will kill and damage our lives. The man's house becomes worse more than before. That's why Jesus said: the wicked generation wants to bring evil spirit into their lives to control and destroy every man's life. We can give our hearts to Jesus and ask Him to make us strong in faith.

"Then he goes and takes with him seven other spirits more wicked than himself, and they enter and dwell there; and the last state of that man is worse than the first. So shall it also be with this wicked generation." Matthew 12:38-45, NKJV.

Jesus' Mother and Brothers: Jesus was still there to teach the multitudes, and they were all listing to the beautiful Words of Him. He didn't know that His mother and His brothers were there waiting outside to see Him. Someone came to Him, Your mother and Your brothers are searching for you to speak with you. He answered him to the one who told Jesus. **"Who is My mother, and who are My brothers?"** Matthew 12:48, NKJV. He just stretched out His hands toward His disciples. He said to them, whoever follows my Words and to do the will of my Father is my brother, my sister, and my mother.

"For whoever does the will of My Father in heaven is My brother and sister and mother." Matthew 12:46-50, NKJV.

Wheat and Weeds in the Field: Jesus pointed out that the Kingdom of Heaven is like a man who went to sow good seed in his field. While he was sleeping, the enemy came to sow weeds among the wheat on the ground, and the enemy fled away. After a while, all seeds began to grow with weeds and to grain wheat together to produce a harvest. Then His servants came to the owner of the field; Sir, did you sow a good seed on the ground, but how does it the wheat has weeds grow up beside it. He said: the enemy has done such things.

The servants said to him; Do you want us to gather all weeds out of the field? The owner said:

No, let it be just like this! Let wheat and weeds all grow up together to the time of harvest, and I will tell reapers to separate them the weeds from the wheat. First, bind them all weeds together and burn them. And in the time of harvest, all wheat crop gathered them and will take them to my barn.

Here is the meaning of the parable: The Kingdom of heaven is a man who sowed a seed is: the Son of Man. The field represents the world. Good seed will be as children of the kingdom or the children of God. We can describe weeds as the enemy; also, it will be the children of evil. We can represent the harvest at the end of the world. We can explain the reapers as the angels.

"Let both grow together until the harvest, and at the time of harvest, I will say to the reapers. First, gather together the tares and bind them in bundles to burn them but gather the wheat into my barn." Matthew 13:24-30, NKJV.

The Seed Sown in the Heart: Jesus taught people with a parable, He said: there was a farmer who went to spread his seeds in the fields.

1. Some seeds fell to the wayside, but some birds came down to eat seeds up.

2. Some other seeds fell on the rocky areas in the fields. But it didn't have much heavy soil to grow. When the sun came over the fields, it didn't make strong roots and dried them out quickly.

3. Other seeds fell on thorns and grow up to make very good plants.

4. And last seeds fell on the good ground has good soil. It is making an excellent root to grow. It produces a hundred, sixty, or thirty times what have sown on the ground.

Jesus will reveal the parable here that there are four seeds for four kinds of persons. The seed represents the Word of God.

First: The seed sows in the heart of a first-person will hear the Word. He is interested in the beginning, but later on; He ignores it, which he heard before. The pleasure of the world will take away the seed out of his heart. **"And as he sowed, some seed fell by the wayside; and the birds came and devoured them."** Matthew 13:4. NKJV.

Second: It plants the Word on the second person's heart who will hear the Word. The heart is open to understanding and will accept the Word. During living in the world, having more challenges, and struggling in life. The Word is not affecting not much in the heart of a man because of the troubles of daily life. The person will not allow the Word making a good root in his heart, and he loses the Word. **"Some fell on stony places, where they did not have much earth; and they immediately sprang up because they had no depth of earth."** Matthew 13:5, NKJV.

Third: The Word came in the heart; it made a root to have faith in the Christian life. But after a while, the heart was not hungry to receive it fully. The problem of the world came to take away the seed out of the person's life. It became a strong root for a short while, later on, the person loses his interest to follow God. **"And some fell among thorns, and the thorns sprang up and choked them."** Matthew 13:7, NKJV.

Four: The Word is sown on the good soil in the last person's heart. The heart represents a field. He heard the Word, received with all his heart. His heart was hungry and made a good root. The Spirit of God pours in as the Living Water. It's making an excellent fruit in life and will never lose his faith and his harvest. Jesus said: some produce a hundredfold, some sixty, some thirty. He who has ears, let them hear the Word of God. **"But others fell on good ground and yielded a**

crop: some a hundredfold, some sixty, some thirty." Matthew 13:8, NKJV.

Anytime the Word of God is preached, the Word will be planted in the heart of any man who hears the Word. It is just like a farmer scattering the seed in the field. The heart of a man is open to understand and accept the Word. It will grow and bring harvest and blessings. **"He who has ears to hear, let him hear!"** Matthew 13:9, NKJV.

The Purpose of Parables: The disciples wandered and asked of Him, why do you talk to us in parables, He said to them; because I have given the secret of the kingdom of heaven to you that you may experience it. But it has not given to them, for whoever belief which will be given more to him. And he will have plenty.

But whoever appears to have everything, even though what he has, it will be taken away from him. Jesus said: I have to speak with many who can have eyes to see the Kingdom of God and ready to hear the Good News and to understand the eternal life is near to them. Jesus spoke with a simple parable to explain many stories with an easy illustration. He makes a truthful statement to accept the love of God.

"Therefore, I speak to them in parables, because seeing they do not see, and hearing they do not hear, nor do they understand." Matthew 13:10-13, NKJV.

Hidden Treasure: This parable of the 'hidden treasure' will teach us to seek the revelation of the Kingdom of God is near to us. The kingdom is so precious that we cannot understand its value that is above anything else. The meaning of the parable is about a man who sold all he had to keep the kingdom. The treasure describes Jesus, the Savior, and He brings redemption to humankind. The treasures are revealing the true divinity of God.

"Again, the kingdom of heaven is like treasure hidden in a field, which a man found and hid; and for joy over it he goes and sells all that he has and buys that field." Matthew 13:44, NKJV.

Pearl of Great Price: Look at the merchant kept seeking pearls when he noticed one pearl has a high value. While we cannot purchase salvation and pay for the forgiveness of our own sins, we cannot exchange an eternal life by our worldly things. Later, we will identify the pearl is also Jesus and a new life; it prepares us to give up all things to follow Him. No one can find the knowledge and authority of God by worldly intelligence. We must seek Him through His Word. We receive the love of God, and eternal life through Christ shall be given to us by faith.

"Again, the kingdom of heaven is like a merchant seeking beautiful pearls, who, when he had found one pearl of great price, went and sold all that he had and bought it." Matthew 13:45-46, NKJV.

Divided Bad and Good: Jesus shared another parable; The Kingdom of heaven is like a net which will cast out into the sea. They will be gathering some of several kinds of fish when they get full and brought them to the shore. Then they sat down, they divided them, some were good, and some were bad. The best one kept them into boats, and the one is bad threw them away. The time will come to the near of the age.

There will be weeping and gnashing of teeth, Matthew 8:12, NKJV. The Lord sends the angles that will reach out forth to split the evil among the righteous. They will cast the wicked into the furnace of fire. Jesus said to His disciples, did you understand about these things to come? They said: Yes, Lord. He said: Every teacher of the law who has turned into a follower in the kingdom of heaven. It will be like the householder who brings out of his storeroom new treasures as new and as old.

"So, it will be at the end of the age. The angels will come forth, separate the wicked from among the just, and cast them into the furnace of fire. There will be wailing and gnashing of teeth." Matthew 13:47-52, NKJV.

A Prophet Without Honor: Jesus finished His teaching and healing in other cities. He passed by in His own town Nazareth. He went to start teaching in the synagogue and preaching the Word of God. Everyone who was there listens to His teaching. They all marveled and asked each other. Is He the one who was the son of Joseph from our city? He grew up with his family as we know His father, Joseph, and His mother.

We also know His brothers: James, Joses, Simon, Judas, and his sisters. Where He received all wisdom and knowledge of God? The people of the city knew Jesus's family since He was living in this town. Jesus said:

"But Jesus said to them, A prophet is not without honor except in his own country

and his own house. Now He did not do many mighty works there because of their unbelief." Matthew 13:53-58, NKJV.

Tradition and God's Commands: Some teachers of the Law and Pharisees who were from Jerusalem, when they saw Jesus, they came to Him. Asking Him: We see Your disciples will try to break the tradition of the elders, and they don't want to wash their hands when they eat bread. Jesus said: Why do you like also break the commandment of God because of your practice and tradition? You are declaring as you know the Law.

Is it true as God commanded, saying, **"Honor your father and your mother with respect,"**; and, if he who curses his father or mother not admire them, let him brought in to death. Why do you also not obey the Law, which was given to you? Jesus said: You are Hypocrites! Rightly did Isaiah prophesy about you, saying:

"These people draw near to Me with their mouth, And honor Me with their lips, But their heart is far from Me. And in vain they worship Me, Teaching as doctrines the commandments of men." Matthew 15:1-9, NKJV.

What Comes Out of the Heart: Jesus describes here about "defilement" is being morally wrong or such an impurity, degraded, or perverted. To defile a body is an act of extreme grief toward God and will separate everything around. Sin can corrupt a man, a society, or a population.

When Jesus called the multitude to himself. He shared about; what goes into the man's mouth, will not defile a man, but what comes out of him, it will defile a man. Jesus's disciples came to Him; they said: "Did you know the Pharisees heard your teaching, they got offended." Jesus answered, leave them alone, they are blind, they will lead blinds, then they both fall into a ditch. One of the disciples of Jesus came to Him, said, teach us to understand the parable.

Jesus taught the Word; what goes into the mouth of any man will not defile him, but what comes out of his heart defiles a man. He said: what comes out of the heart: evil purposes or bad thoughts, murders, infidelities, sexual intercourse, robberies, dishonest witness, blasphemies. These things will defile a man; even Jesus said: if unwashed hands will not defile a man.

"For out of the heart proceed evil thoughts, murders, adulteries, fornications, thefts, false

witness, blasphemies." Matthew 15:10-20, NKJV.

The Leaven, Pharisees, and Sadducees: Jesus made this illustration to give us an understanding of how we can recognize the religious doctrine. Let's look at the meaning of "The Leaven" or "The Yeast" is a type of misery and corruption. He points out to the Pharisees and Sadducees. Jesus made a clear view of their culture and teaching about "yeast." Because of a small part of wrong teaching can affect a large group of communities to believe the incorrect thing. It will not accomplish the message of the kingdom of God.

Jesus wanted to preach the Salvation of God, and His teaching should be from the truth of God's Word. As 'yeast' functions until the bread becomes fully risen, the ultimate preaching of the kingdom of God will be global.

There are differences between the doctrine of the Pharisees and the Sadducees throughout the Scriptures. The Sadducees denied a concept of the resurrection of the dead, but the Pharisees appeared to agree on the resurrection. The Sadducees accepted the Hebrew Bible but rejected the instructions of the Pharisees in connection with the experience that observed the Bible and oral law. "The deity and spirit of the Oral Law as passed on from God to Moses on Mount Sinai." Sadducees denied the doctrine of any kind of existence after death, but the Pharisees recognize a resurrection, and angels, demons, heaven, and hell.

The character of the yeast is to develop and to transform whatever it approaches a higher level. That's why the message of the Good News can be remarkable. When we receive Jesus, His grace increases in our spirits and shapes us from the inside out. As the truth of God comes and will live in our hearts. It applies an omnipresent Word of the Living God, as we see His manifestation of His glory. We acknowledge that we are created into his image with a forever-growing splendor, which takes place from the Lord.

"Then they understood that He did not tell them to beware of the leaven of bread, but of the doctrine of the Pharisees and Sadducees." Matthew 16:5-12, NKJV.

Pick Up the Cross and Follow Him: Jesus inspired everyone who chooses to follow him. He said: if you desire to come into my kingdom, you need to leave all worldly ambition behind. Set aside every human's temptation to believe in Jesus and carry the cross. I believe we must have an eagerness to die in ourselves, then the fruits of spirit would come to give us new peace, joy in the Holy Spirit.

We desire to complete surrender onto Him. He replied, for whoever chooses to take care of his own life will lose it, but anyone who gives up his life for me will save it. What profit is it for a fellow man to win the entire world and yet lose himself?

Accepting Jesus is easy for everyone, but when we want to follow Jesus, it will be challenging to walk with Jesus during a trial of life. A true believer would declare his faith with a genuine pledge to himself would say, I follow Jesus, no turning back to the world again. Christian will go through tests, but Jesus encouraged us that prosecutions will happen to His followers.

If we believe, we are ready to pick up our cross daily, look at these challenges in the Christian life:

-if we lose members of our families?
-if we lose our possession?
-if we go through the failure of life?
-if we lose our profession?
-if we lose our health?

Are we still eager to follow Jesus? The Lord Jesus will strengthen us to take up our cross and to move forward with Him. There is "A Call" in everyone's life:

We are called:

To walk with Him.

To worship and honor Him.

To serve Him.

To become a follower of Christ.

To witness His name to many lost souls.

To have peace, joy in the Holy Spirit.

To have eternal life with the Lord Jesus.

When we pick up our cross every day, we grow in our faith to go beyond what we usually believed to become desirable. He is always faithful; He never wishes to fail us and forsake us. We will rejoice in His presence, and we receive our everlasting reward.

"For the Son of Man will come in the glory of His Father with His angels, and then He will reward each according to his works. Assuredly, I say to you, there are some standing here who shall not taste death till they see the Son of Man coming in His kingdom." Matthew 16:24-28, NKJV.

Who Is the Greatest?: The disciples came to Jesus, asked Him: Who will be the greatest in the kingdom of heaven? He responded to have a little child come to Him; he sat down in the midst of them. He said: unless you humble yourself to become just like a small child is the greatest in the kingdom of heaven. I will assure you; you will enter the Kingdom of God.

Jesus said: You receive a little child in my name; you receive me. Receiving Jesus needed to have a simple faith and believing that He is the Son of God, and He is the Savior of the World. The reason Jesus said you have to become as a little child means: A small child is innocent and precious in God's eyes.

"Therefore, whoever humbles himself as this little child is the greatest in the kingdom of heaven." Matthew 18:1-5, NKJV.

Jesus Warns of Offenses: Here in this message, Jesus had just strengthened His followers against any of their lust ambitions. So, He recommended that anyone who does sins. He gave a good sample about if one of your eyes causes you to sin, which you might consider to take one eye out, not to lead you to hell. When Jesus encourages us to look at ourselves where sins planted?

He said, whatever sin is trying to make you do wrongdoing if your eyes cause you trouble to carry sins in your life. It's needed to pluck out a sinful eye, and it may cut off a reckless part of your body.

We need to realize if sin draws every man to hell and that sin causes us not to come into the Life of Jesus. We have to escape the danger of everlasting tormented hell, but we receive Jesus by faith, we can enter into His eternal life.

Men are tempted and attracted to sin as a growing motive. Every person would like to choose for themselves is the start point of sinning. Every sin produces a lousy heart that will lead to a bad attitude or behavior that starts with a desire. We must remember every desire itself is not wrong, and with many great passions can lead to blessings. But the human's choices that move us into sin become a terrible ambition.

It based on the needs of having the right attitude and putting our faith in believing the Word of God. We need to get rid of an undesirable character. We must put the desire of God first and recognizing the plan of God. Then we follow Jesus what it takes us to eternity.

"If your hand or foot causes you to sin, cut it off and cast it from you. It is better for you

to enter into life lame or maimed, rather than having two hands or two feet, to be cast into the everlasting fire. And if your eye causes you to sin, pluck it out and cast it from you. It is better for you to enter into life with one eye, rather than having two eyes, to be cast into hell fire." Matthew 18:6-9, NKJV.

The Lost Sheep Found: Jesus describes you, do not neglect one of these precious little ones. Their angels will always see the Father's face in heaven. There will be a parable explain the sheep, which was lost. There is a man who has a hundred sheep; he will take care of his sheep; one of them ran off got separated from other sheep. Jesus said: do you think? The man will not leave the ninety-nine sheep and goes around, looking for the one which was lost. He will find it and bringing back, rejoicing over the one was lost but now is found.

Jesus said: It is not the Father's will who is in heaven that none of these sheep will perish. The Son of Man came to save and restore the one who was lost; now, he shall be found.

"And if he should find it, assuredly, I say to you, he rejoices more over that sheep than over

the ninety-nine that did not go astray." Matthew 18:10-14, NKJV.

Handling with a Sinning Brother: How can we handle a brother's sin in the body of Christ? When Jesus mentioned, If your brother or sister has committed sins, you may go to discuss the situation just between two of you. If they would be interested in listening to you, you have restored them for the Lord. But if they will not accept your discussion with them. You may allow taking your concern to one or two other witnesses in the church. So, it may establish every spiritual conversation in the presence of the Lord by two or three witnesses. If they still want to ignore or even reject to accept their sins.

In this situation, you may report to the church; and if they still not accept the church's advice. Jesus said you might hold them accountable for their behaviors as you would treat them as a pagan worshipper or a tax collector. We as Christians always prefer to handle conflicts in love, with the hope of rebuilding a believer's life.

Most people agree that we can sin that would be all right to enjoy our way of sinful attitude while we are living in Christ. Others will see which sins have committed, and another believer will not pay attention to any wrongdoing in life. It should be prayer useful to our spiritual understanding, and we trust the scriptural truths. However, there are some occasions when an individual will get counseling becomes an important step.

We will handle any conflict by prayer to the Lord. We pray for blessings and moving forward with a wise solution that supports a person's spiritual growth. We wish the persons' life turned around into good faith.

"But if he will not hear, take with you one or two more, that by the mouth of two or three witnesses every word may be established. And if he refuses to hear them, tell it to the church. But if he refuses even to hear the church, let him be to you like a heathen and a tax collector." Matthew 18:15-17, NKJV.

Unforgiving Servant Will Pay: In this parable, we will look at unmerciful servants. One of the disciples of Jesus, Peter came to Him, asked Him: How many times I must forgive my brothers and my sisters if they have sinned against me, up to seventy times? Jesus answered him: No! Not seventy times, but seventy-seven times.

He shared about: A servant has owed the king ten thousand bags of gold, for the servant was a huge debt, how he could pay back to the King. So, the king wanted to arrange with his servant, who owed him bags of gold. He called him, and he found out. He cannot repay him, so the king ordered to capture all his possessions, his family, his wife, all his children to be sold to repay his debt.

The servant realized that he would lose everything. He fell down on his knees in front of the king. He begged the king to be patient with him; he will pay him back. The king had mercy on him; let him go and canceled his debt.

When the servant got out, and he went to get in touch with his fellow servant who owed him one hundred denarii. He took him by his hands and held his hand on his throat. He said: You must pay me what you owed. The fellow servant fell down on his knees, asked him to be patient with him, and he pays him back. He had no mercy on him; He took him into prison.

So, the King's servants have seen this situation, and they came to the king. They reported to the king what has happened to the servant who mistreated other fellow servants and took him into prison.

The king called the servant; asked him, why did you not have mercy on your fellow servant. I have been compassionate to you, and I decided to let you go, why you didn't want to be merciful toward others. The king got angry; he handed him over to torture him. He will learn his mistake until the servant will pay all his debt. Jesus said: If you don't forgive your brothers with their sins, my Heavenly Father will do to you.

"So, My heavenly Father also will do to you if each of you, from his heart, does not forgive his brother his trespasses." Matthew 18:21-35, NKJV.

Marriage and Divorce: God created a marriage union in the creation. He established with Adam and Eve, which is a relationship between man and woman unified. When God put two together, do not let man separate them from each other. The Bible answers with sufficiently evident that God has not designed divorce. He hates it. But He made them, man and woman, to become one flesh, and they shall be joint together. He prepared them with love and harmony. God created them to multiply populations on the earth.

However, God allows that separation will take place, even in the time of Moses has permitted in the Old Testament among the children of Israel. Today marriage can happen everywhere and is not honored and not respected among God's people. Jesus explains that divorce is a compromise to man's sin that opposes God's purpose. He made a marriage covenant and bonded them jointly.

God blessed them that they could be fruitful from all races, colors, cultures, and covered the earth. The time God had formed man and woman together. Because of God's plan would allow sexuality performed between one man and one woman in the holy covenant of marriage only. We study the Word, which is telling us that outside of marriage, human lust is a serious interest, and it becomes higher than any other sinful desire which draws us to perish.

"He said to them, "Moses, because of the hardness of your hearts, permitted you to divorce your wives, but from the beginning, it was not so. And I say to you, whoever divorces his wife, except for sexual immorality, and marries another, commits adultery; and whoever marries her who is divorced commits adultery." Matthew 19:1-10, NKJV.

Jesus Teaches on Celibacy: Jesus points out that most people usually do not wish to get married, and they want to become a celibate for life. Some people were born to be a celibate. As we learn, the Bible does not explicitly say; this is "the gift of celibacy." But it goes on to reveal that God gives strength and living singleness to be willing to serve others and God. He provides the grace for being a celibate to walk in obedience by serving God. He offers a reward to those who follow His plan.

Most people will have a desire to get married, and this need is not leading to sin. In fact, it is a holy covenant of marriage that can protect us from sin. Every man and woman should have their own partners as one husband and one wife.

Some people would rather than participating in wrongdoing with other unfaithful relationships with the opposite sex. The Word said, the Christian believers are to be married, and this is God's plan. Some feel it is A Call from the Lord Jesus to serve Him. Celibacy is a gift for some men or women, but there will not be for everyone. Most people are seeking to get married.

Apostle Paul said if some people having a desire to get married is not sin. God established a family is an essential part of the human being.

However, some will wait upon God for a short time then they will get married later. Whereas for some others will seek God's direction to get married or not? Some will remain celibate for their lifetime, and they will receive happiness with great satisfaction to serve God and the church.

"For there are eunuchs who were born thus from their mother's womb, and there are eunuchs who were made eunuchs by men, and there are eunuchs who have made themselves eunuchs for the kingdom of heaven's sake. He who is able to accept it, let him accept it." Matthew 19:11-12, NKJV.

Not Easy to Enter the kingdom of God: There was a young man came to Jesus, he asked Him: I have kept the law of God since I was a youth, what do I need to do more? Jesus answered: If you want to be a perfect man because you have kept all these things from your youth. You may go, after that, sell your possessions and give them to the poor. Then you can have treasures in heaven, come and follow Me. The young man heard, he was not happy, because he had a great possession, he did not want to give his possessions to the poor to follow Jesus.

Jesus said: **"it is easier for a camel to go through the eye of a needle than for a rich man to enter the kingdom of God."** Matthew 19:20-24, NKJV.

With God, All Things Are Possible: What does the Word means: "with God, all things are possible?" We read His Word said, God can save sinners only, and He will give them everlasting life. There are no human being can make it possible by any other power to forgive sins. The salvation of God has happened by the willingness of His Son Jesus on the cross. Therefore, what should be our reaction to this invitation of God? He wants us to be humbled under His presence and to have a submission to His Word. He wants us to trust Him for the rest of our lives. Then we will know, "Nothing is impossible with God."

His disciples asked: Lord, who can be saved? Peter said we left everything to follow you. What we have now? So Jesus said to them, surely I declare to you when the Son of Man sits on the throne of His majesty. Those who have accepted Me will likewise be granted to sit on the twelve thrones will judge the twelve tribes of Israel. And anybody who has given up brothers, sisters, father, mother, wife, children, houses, lands, for

My name's sake, shall receive a hundredfold. Jesus said, those who are first, shall be last, and those who last will be first.

"And everyone who has left houses or brothers or sisters or father or mother or wife or children or lands, for My name's sake, shall receive a hundredfold, and inherit eternal life. But many who are first will be last, and the last first." Matthew 19:25-30, NKJV.

Workers in the Vineyard: In this parable, we learn how to enter the Kingdom of God, will have a privilege to serve, and work for the Lord. The landowner tried to hire laborers to work in his unique vineyard. He thought to go to the marketplace to find workers in the early morning around six. He found the first group of workers; He offered them the wage one denarius. They accepted the work and the wage. They came to start working in the vineyard. After three hours later, around nine, the landowner went to the marketplace again to hire more workers. This second group came to work and agreed to receive one denarius wage.

The landowner went at noon and three in the afternoon to the marketplace to find more workers; They were standing and waiting that someone would come to hire them. He asked, what are you doing here; you would come to work in my vineyard. Again, the landowner went on his last trip to the marketplace at five in the afternoon. He saw, there were still workers standing doing nothing, he asked; What are you doing here, you may come, work in my vineyard?

Now the day of working was ended at six is almost the day is over. The landowner asked his steward to give these workers their wages. The landowner said: let's start paying the last workers who came at five in the afternoon. So, the steward gave them one denarius. He gave them all the groups their wages who came later. It came to pay wages to the first group began to work in the early morning at the same wages, one denarius.

They began to complain about it. They said; we arrived very early morning to work, the last group came at five in the afternoon. They worked for one hour only, and they received the same wages as we received. We should get more payments than them because we came to work very early morning. The landowner said: we agreed that your wages would be one denarius; they said: Yes. He said to them, get your wage and go your way. The landowner said: I make the right decision for myself, whatever I will choose with my own money!

Jesus said: remember the last shall be first, and the first shall be last. He will tell us that those people are entering the Kingdom of God at the last moment. They will receive a reward of salvation and entering the Kingdom of God by Grace. And those first have entered the Kingdom of God; it will be given at the same reward. They will have everlasting life.

Jesus said again: Many will hear the Word, they will be called to enter the Kingdom of God, but few are chosen.

"So, the last will be first, and the first last. For many are called, but few chosen." Matthew 20:1-16, NKJV.

Greatness is Serving: There is a beautiful story that has happened where the mother of Zebedee's sons came to Jesus, kneeling down and asking Him. She said to Jesus; Please grant my two sons may sit, one son, will sit at Your right hand and the other son sit at your left in Your kingdom. He answered; you do not know what are you asking for? Are you ready to drink the cup, and to suffer for the sin of the world, and are you prepared to die for humankind? My Father He who had made the right plan, not me. The Kingdom works with a unique set of rules.

We cannot find greatness in wealth.

We cannot find greatness in popularity.

We cannot find greatness in position.

We cannot find greatness in authority.

We cannot find greatness in intelligence.

We find greatness in serving in the Kingdom of Jesus. We cannot find greatness in being served, but we can find greatness in helping others only.

If we are going to grow into the greatest among Christian believers, then we are ready to minister God's family. But Jesus showed us the Way to remind us to humble ourselves to the pathway of obedience. The Way of Jesus is better to take us to glory. His path will lead us to honor and in serving God's people. We will take pleasure in serving God; that is our greatness. Jesus said I came to serve the entire world but not to be served.

"Yet it shall not be so among you; but whoever desires to become great among you, let him be your servant. And whoever desires to be first among you, let him be your slave, just as the Son of Man did not come to be served,

but to serve, and to give His life a ransom for many." Matthew 20:20-28, NKJV.

The Two Sons: We see in the parable that there was a man had two sons, and the father went to his first son, asked him: would you go to my vineyard to work there! The son said, I will not, but later on, he changed his mind; he went to work in the vineyard. The father went to his second son, asked him, would you go to my vineyard to work there, the son said: I will go, but later he didn't go. Then Jesus asked them, which of one of these two sons did the will of the father? They answered: The first son!

Surely, I declare to you that tax collectors and prostitutes will accept and will enter the kingdom of God before you. When John came in the way of righteousness, you have rejected him. Those people have accepted and have believed John. But you have heard him and saw him, and you still have not believed yet.

"For John came to you in the way of righteousness, and you did not believe him, but tax collectors and harlots believed him; and when you saw it, you did not afterward relent and believe him." Matthew 21:28-32, NKJV.

Wicked Vinedressers in the Vineyard: There was a landowner who planted a vineyard; he dug a winepress. He made a wall surrounded his vineyard with a tower. He wanted to travel to a far country. He rented his vineyard to vinedressers to take care of it for him. When the vintage time came near, he tried to get fruit out of his vineyard. He sent his servants to the vineyard to get some fruit. So, vinedressers saw them, beat one of them, killed another one, and they stoned the other one. The landowner sent more servants to the vineyard to get fruits.

The vinedressers did, at the same, likewise to the first group of servants. The landowner thought I would send my son, and it might be good they will respect my son; they give fruits to him. He sent his son; they saw his son came for asking for the fruit of the vineyard. They said to themselves. He is the heir, let's also kill him, and destroy his inheritance. They attacked him, casting him out of the vineyard, and killed him.

Jesus asked: what do you think the landowner will do to these vinedressers. They answered Him: He will demolish those wicked vinedressers. He will find other vinedressers to take care of it and to receive more fruits. He said: have you heard: the house built on the stone, but it will be rejected. Jesus is the chief cornerstone of the foundation of the church. He said: The kingdom of God will be taken away from you and given to others for bearing more fruits. Is anyone who falls on this stone will be crush to pieces.

"The stone which the builders rejected, has become the chief cornerstone. This was the Lord's doing, and it is marvelous in our eyes?" Matthew 21:33-42, NKJV.

Guests at the Wedding Banquet: There is an excellent story about the Kingdom of God is like a King who has a son to prepare a wedding banquet for him. As we know, the King is God, who will make a banquet for His Son Jesus. Let's look at this parable together.

The King will send out his servants to invite many quests for the wedding. But these quests were not interested in attending the banquet. The King sent out another servant to those quests that said: I have already prepared a good dinner with fatted cattle with great dishes, and dinner is ready for you. Some quests were busy with their own business, and working with their farms and families. These quests were attacked the King's servants, killed them all. When the King discovered what had taken place to his servants were all killed. He organized his armies to attack them back to those killers to destroy and burned their cities.

Then the King said to his servants, the wedding is ready therefore go to the city street, find people as many as you can, invite them to the wedding. So, those King's servants went to the street, found many were good or bad, they invited them into the wedding. The banquet hall was full of quests. The moment the King arrived to meet all the quests, he saw a man was standing and didn't have a wedding garment on! He asked him, Have you come to the banquet without a wedding garment. The man looked at the King, but he did not answer to the King. And the king ordered his servants to bind his hands, his foot, take him away, put him outside into the darkness, there can be a place weeping and gnashing of teeth.

Now the parable means: The King represents God; the banquet held for His Son Jesus. Those servants would speak the Good News as prophets and preachers. They preached the Word, but those quests as the people will not accept the invitation. They will be rejecting the message of God. So, they invited ordinary people from the street, and they received a call at the wedding.

Those people become as the children or people of God.

There was a man who did not have a garment, but he attended the wedding. It means that he just came by himself, but he didn't accept God as the King. That's why the King looked at him, and he didn't wear on the wedding garment. The garment can represent as the Grace of God or the salvation of God. The King ordered to throw him out of the wedding. It may happen too many people in the time of judgment.

Jesus said: **"For many are called, but few are chosen."** Matthew 22:1-14, NKJV.

Paying Taxes to Caesar or Not? Jesus gave them an outstanding answer to the questions of the Pharisees about paying taxes. He did wonderfully explains to the lawmakers, and Jesus gave them a precise answer, how to pay your taxes in the right way. They were trying to trap Jesus into His speech and making things illegal. Then the Pharisees confronted him: Do we need to pay taxes to Caesar or not? They have thought maybe Jesus could give them the right answer. They wanted Jesus would be accountable for paying taxes. Jesus could surely not neglect to pay taxes to an authority like Rome, which was severe.

But Jesus looked at them through their theories and showed them an excellent explain: "give to Caesar are Caesar's, and to God is God's." Jesus taught a meaningful message. Money can be an earthly thing; it will bring temporary pleasure and is a contrast to the kingdom of God. Jesus understands that we have an obligation on two stages to both; first to support the church which belongs to God and second to support a governmental authority is the land where we live.

"And He said to them, "Render therefore to Caesar the things that are Caesar's, and to God the things that are God's." When they had heard these words, they marveled, and left Him and went their way. " Matthew 22:15-22, NKJV.

The Sadducees asked About the Resurrection? I want to share briefly about the Sanhedrin was the highest court of justice and also the supreme council in ancient Jerusalem. The word Sanhedrin means council or assembly. The supreme council, which had two parties were ruling in the land of Israel in the time of Jesus. These two parties called: The Sadducees and the Pharisees, which had seventy seats both altogether in council. The Sadducees had the majority of the seats in the council, but the Pharisees had minority seats in the council as well.

The Pharisees had a vast majority of Jewish people under their control, and these members of Pharisees influenced the population. These Pharisees generally dominated the rules in the Sanhedrin. Alike even the Sadducees and Pharisees were two different viewpoints of each other concerning their fundamental faith tradition within Judaism. They were obligated to serve jointly together to the Jewish populations.

When we study the Word of God, and we discover many places are talking about the chief priests and the Pharisees. These groups were the chief priests from the members of the Sadducees. Therefore, these groups were the chief priests and the Pharisees cooperating. We still look at the relationship between the priests and the Sadducees described in many situations in the New Testament.

As we pointed out about what their beliefs are: the Pharisees groups and the Sadducee groups developed their own faith doctrine regarding the Torah, which is five books of Moses. These two groups have had two views of the resurrection of death. So, the Sadducees have believed that there was no resurrection after death. But the Pharisees' theory believed in the resurrection.

Jesus Himself debated with the Sadducees in referring to the questioning of the resurrection. They asked Him about a woman who had many husbands, and all of them died. The Sadducees began to ask Jesus about which one of these men would be her an actual husband in the resurrection.

Jesus answered: In the resurrection, they will not join together, and even will not be given in marriage, He said, they will be just like angels of God in heaven. But referring to the resurrection of the dead, have you not read what is revealed to you by God, saying:

"For in the resurrection they neither marry nor are given in marriage, but are like angels of God in heaven. But concerning the resurrection of the dead, have you not read what was spoken to you by God, saying. I am the God of Abraham, the God of Isaac, and the God of Jacob'? God is not the God of the dead, but of the living." Matthew 22:23-33, NKJV.

Which is the First Commandment?: Jesus stated that to love God, passionately must be the first choice and should be the greatest commandment of all. If we sincerely worship God, we will continue performing all the other commandments as becoming the greatest, which follows them all. God himself offered us the essential commandment to love Him, and He provided the different divine rules. This fundamental law applies to describe the essence of obedience in which we must preserve all the commandments. If we are not actively observing one rule, we will not be able actually to keep any of the law either.

We realize this is the first Commandment. Jesus said, "If you surely love me, you will follow my commandments." If we sincerely love God with our hearts, with our souls, and with our minds, it becomes natural to obey His Words. He will take care of us with His grace and mercy to make it easy to walk in His righteousness.

I want to point out here: How we truly love God, it means; praising Him, worshiping Him, adoring Him, and obeying His Word. Our genuine love will give Him our sincere appreciation to His glory, as stated in the Bible.

"Jesus said to him, 'You shall love the Lord your God with all your heart, with all your soul, and with all your mind.' This is the first and great commandment. "

One of the lawmakers asked Jesus a question about the greatest commandment. The motive of the Pharisees appears that when we fail to have an intimacy with God personally, and not to be able to honor him heartily. What shall we do? Are we going back to God again? Jesus has mentioned here; we must have a relationship with Him and love Him in a personal way. Those lawmakers thought following the commandments of God is one of the ritual religions to please God but not with a whole heart.

Jesus said, when you have a love for God, your passion will draw you to obey Him, and you live for God according to His Word. Jesus said about the second commandments,

"You shall love your neighbor as yourself.' On these two commandments hang all the Law and the Prophets." Matthew 22:34-40, NKJV.

How Can David Call His Descendant Lord?:

We read in the book of Matthew will explain to us that Jesus wanted to ask the Pharisees about who is Christ? Whose Son is He? He had one answer, saying, the Son of David! Jesus had challenged the Pharisees to give the right answer that He was the ancestor of David. I believe they heard or had some knowledge of knowing the forefather of Jesus. At the same time, there were ancestors' fathers, there was one that was necessary to the Jews only, and the Pharisees gave with the correct answer. The Bible would tell us that Jesus was a descendant and an offspring of David.

We see in the book of Psalms that King David called for someone else, his Lord. He was pointing out to God of Israel. God revealed the Messiah in the Psalms. King David was related to God as his own Lord. It has mentioned that God leads Israel's enemies into submission and to serve Him. Those Jews found out that Jesus was the Son of God, the King of Jews, to be manifest as the Messiah.

Jesus needed to inform the Pharisees to recognize two facts, that His kingdom is not established on earth, but in heaven! Jesus had to come as the Son of God to earth. He had two characters with fleshly as human and divine nature. We believe Jesus is the Messiah and is also God.

"The Lord said to my Lord, "Sit at My right hand, Till I make Your enemies Your footstool"? If David then calls Him 'Lord,' how is He his Son?" And no one was able to answer Him a word, nor from that day on did anyone

dare question Him anymore." Matthew 22:41-46, NKJV.

Woe to the Scribes and Pharisees: The word Woe, Jesus used is referring to a remark of anguish, tragedy, or misery. There was not the first time Jesus had some sharp comments from the religious lawmakers of His time. Jesus expected the scribes and Pharisees to experience God and to serve the people to teach other parables, learning about the God of Israel. They should suppose to show the way of God, how to follow God's plans. Instead, what they did these religious rulers increased more laws to God's Law, setting up a large ritual. They appeared not to seek God with a sincere heart.

Jesus realized that their doctrine was a ritual for themselves and the people. Well, they established law with a prideful heart. Jesus emphasizes a faithful follower of the Law must be from the word of God. Let's look at why Jesus opposes them so strongly in this situation? Reading at each Woe shows us some understanding.

It makes us recognize that Jesus could have a sharp message for those who stopped people from getting salvation. Their ritual was hindering others from pursuing the Messiah. Jesus rebukes the scribes and Pharisees for making aggressive attempts to gain followers. Later they were taking those followers to misery as the scribes and Pharisees were trying to achieve. However, they had a further purpose in developing their religion than on preserving the faith in a true God.

Jesus tells against the scribes and Pharisees. He says the spiritual rulers that you are "blind guides," and you are just like "blind fools." Then Jesus speaks out about the magnitude of the place of worship and God's holiness.

The Lord Jesus mentioned to the lawmakers that their exercise of faith for giving their offering and the tithe to the temple. But while they would not really pay attention to people. Jesus emphasized, they tried to concentrate on the message of the Law and lived by it with pride heart. But they were missing out on the greatest sincerity and essential things of God. Their ritual, religion designed for showing off, not from their cores of being.

Jesus made a statement on their hypocrisy in the Woe. He wanted to give a message to these Pharisees and scribes. He spoke of the religious rulers; they can act correctly on the outside, but they have rejected the inside of their lives. They represent themselves with spiritual leaders, but they are not entering into the presence of the God of Israel to be true worshipers.

Jesus replies, when you clean up the outside, how about the inside of your life is full of self-ishness, you do not have any kindness toward people. There will be a transformation of new life that would take place from the inside-out to manifest the power of God. Jesus calls for the scribes and Pharisees are presenting their rules with a wonderful glory on the outside with "deception and depravity." They offer themselves to serve, but their hearts are far from God.

Jesus concludes with a harsh word to the religious rulers that they are following, just like their forefathers, who were afflicted with the old prophets. Setting up a stone to the prophets, they swear against themselves, and simply declaring that it was their forefathers who executed the prophets.

I want to add these scriptures of Jesus's Woe from the Book of Matthew chapter 23:

- **"But woe to you, scribes and Pharisees, hypocrites! For you shut up the kingdom of heaven against men; for you neither go in yourselves, nor do you allow those who are entering to go in."** Matthew 23:13, NKJV.

- "Woe to you, scribes and Pharisees, hypocrites! For you devour widows' houses, and for a pretense make long prayers. Therefore you will receive greater condemnation." Matthew 23:14, NKJV.

- "Woe to you, scribes and Pharisees, hypocrites! For you travel land and sea to win one proselyte, and when he is won, you make him twice as much a son of hell as yourselves." Matthew 23:15, NKJV.

- "Woe to you, blind guides, who say, 'Whoever swears by the temple, it is nothing; but whoever swears by the gold of the temple, he is obliged to perform it.' Fools and blind! For which is greater, the gold or the temple that sanctifies the gold?" Matthew 23:16-17, NKJV.

- "Woe to you, scribes and Pharisees, hypocrites! For you pay tithe of mint and anise and cummin, and have neglected the weightier matters of the law: justice and mercy and faith. These you ought to have done, without leaving the others undone." Matthew 23:23, NKJV.

- "Woe to you, scribes and Pharisees, hypocrites! For you cleanse the outside of the cup and dish, but inside they are full of extortion and self-indulgence. Blind Pharisee, first cleanse the inside of the cup and dish, that the outside of them may be clean also." Matthew 23:25-26, NKJV.

- "Woe to you, scribes and Pharisees, hypocrites! For you are like whitewashed tombs which indeed appear beautiful outwardly, but inside are full of dead men's bones and all uncleanness. Even so you also outwardly appear righteous to men, but inside you are full of hypocrisy and lawlessness." Matthew 23:27-28, NKJV.

- "Woe to you, scribes and Pharisees, hypocrites! Because you build the tombs of the prophets and adorn the monuments of the righteous, and say, 'If we had lived in the days of our fathers, we would not have been partakers with them in the blood of the prophets.'" Matthew 23:29-30, NKJV.

The Budding Fig Tree: Now, let's understand this parable from the fig tree. When we see a branch becomes tender and brings forth leaves, you know that summer is near. When spring takes place, and the trees grow out fresh leaves, we recognize the new season is here. Jesus has already assured us of His return, and it is getting fulfilled. The fig tree to emphasize a time of His Second coming. In the same manner, we will realize Christ's return is near when we look at the circumstances. He points out a sign of His coming to appear.

Jesus is certainly making a prophecy; He is telling of forthcoming events. Jesus said in His remark, **"I say to you, this generation will by no means pass away till all these things take place,"** Matthew 24:34, NKJV. Already the manifestation of the end appears to us. The "End Time" is on the way and coming soon. His Second coming and the judgment will take place. Those who heard the Good News of Jesus are still living on the earth, thus will have time to give their hearts to Jesus. In fact, they would have a short time to decide to believe Jesus by faith to get saved by the Blood of the Lamb of God. Then the time is getting shorter for them. Jesus said:

"Heaven and earth will pass away, but My words will by no means pass away." Matthew 24:35, NKJV.

The Faithful and the Evil Servant: In this parable, we learn about the wise and evil servants. These two servants were; one was genuine, and the other one was dishonest servants. Both of them called to follow the order of their master to serve in the house of God. The master has called these servants to be truthful and sensible to carrying out their duties to work. A good servant had responsibilities to lead and serve his master's kingdom.

While the Master was away, then He will come back to reward his servants with more works. The Master will assign them to be the ruler of another house of God. Jesus instructs them, and they had to make a good relationship with other fellow believers in the body of Christ.

In this text, Jesus used the word "wise" means: with good judgment, reasonable, sober, realistic. It represents an awareness of people with their conditions, offering individual discernment, and understanding how handling with them.

This parable relates to anybody who loves to be a wise servant. Jesus admonishes us to bring every believer together and strengthens each other. We will motivate others to be a passionate person. We do this by giving those who are seeking the truth. The Lord wants us to live with a good example and encourage others. In this manner, we grow into spiritual awareness and with a faithful servant lifestyle.

It shows the deceitful servant who says to himself that His Master is coming late. His heart turned into a cold spirit, and he became too weak as he began to eat and to grow into drinking. The evil servant's philosophy is arrogant, deceptive, cruel, self-tolerant, and excessive greed. Because he thinks he may have enough time to make a relationship with God, but his attitude turns into more evils.

If we truly trust Jesus that He will come back to us soon. This parable teaches that our spiritual knowledge will improve our lives. He is protecting us from every evil thought. He will not allow us to become wicked servants if we believe that he has chosen us to be His child and a good servant. We have to decide to follow His goodness. He will never let us down. He receives all the glory and honor for Himself. Jesus said: do not live with hypocrites attitude, but continue with a humble spirit will lead us to our destiny.

"the master of that servant will come on a day when he is not looking for him and at an hour that he is not aware of and will cut him in two and appoint him his portion with the hypocrites. There shall be weeping and gnashing of teeth." Matthew 24:45-51, NKJV.

Ten Wise and Foolish Virgins:

In this dynamic illustration of the return of Jesus and all believers were looking forward to meeting their bridegroom to return to the church. We see in this parable that Jesus mentioned: there were ten virgins, five wise and five foolish, they had their lamps with them. They went out to meet the bridegroom. And these five foolish virgins had no oil with them to meet the bridegroom. So, these wise virgins who took more oil with their vessels along with their lamps.

At midnight, they all heard that the bridegroom is coming; they all went out to meet the bridegroom. All virgins got up and took their lamps to go to meet Him. The foolish virgins realized that they run out of oil for their lamps, they asked wise virgins; We are running out of the lamp's oil, would you give us more oil for our lamps?

The wise virgins said: no, we cannot do it, we don't have enough for ourselves. But you go and find the place where they sell oil and buying oil lamps by yourself. Meanwhile, these foolish virgins went out to find oil and buying for themselves. The bridegroom arrived, and those wise virgins went with Him to the wedding, and suddenly, the door got closed on them.

After a while, those foolish came back from buying their oil lamps, they noticed that the bridegroom came already, and they all went with

Him to the wedding. They asked; Please open the door for us, the Lord answered: surely, I don't know you! Therefore, watch the time and hour of the Son of Man is coming!

The bridegroom represents Jesus, and His Church will define in the New Testament as the bride of Christ. Those five wise virgins a picture of Christian believers who love Jesus, they had a good faith and a warm relationship with Jesus. They were excited to meet their Savior in their hearts.

But those foolish virgins were representing non-warm or lukewarm Christian believers, and they may call themselves believers. They wanted to be around those wise virgins, which is an image of pretending and having faith as they are Christians. But they were not born-again Christians. That's why; The Lord said: I don't know you?

"But he answered and said, Assuredly, I say to you, I do not know you. Watch therefore, for you know neither the day nor the hour in which the Son of Man is coming." Matthew 25:1-13, NKJV.

Talents Making More Profits: There was a wealthy man who had three servants; they were trustworthy to him. He chose them and entrusted them. He gave to his first servant five talents, the second servant gave two talents, and the third servant gave one talent before he will be taking off to a far country. The wealthy man wanted them to make these talents to put into the trading business to make more profit. When he comes back, he will get more profit out of his talents.

So, the first man got his five talents; he went put his talents into business, making double and made five talents more. The second man who got two talents, at the same, put his two talents into business, made two more talents. And a third person who got one talent, he was afraid to use it and not putting into the market. He hid it, dug it underground to make sure is safe when his lord comes back to give it back to him.

After a long time, the wealthy man came back home from his journey, and he called all his three servants to himself. He asked the first man who had five talents: he brought five talents more profit to his lord. He said to his servant well done; you were very faithful with small things; you will be given more responsibility to rule over many things.

The second man came to him who had two talents, brought two more talents profit. At the same reward, the wealthy man gave to the first man, gave the second man as well. But a third man came to him; he said I knew you were a difficult man! I was afraid to make any problem for you and myself. Therefore, I hid your talents what is yours, and I bring it back to you.

The wealthy man said: you are a lazy and a wicked man, you did not know how to use your talents, even you didn't take your talent to the bank to make an interest profit out of it. He said: take his talent from him, give it to the man who has ten talents will know what to do! Jesus said: to those who have talents, it will be given much more. But to those who have it and not knowing what to do with talents, it will be taken away from them what they have, and it will be given to others. Jesus said again: It will come a time for those unprofitable men will be cast out into darkness place; there will be weeping and gnashing teeth.

"For to everyone who has, more will be given, and he will have abundance; but from him who does not have, even what he has will be taken away. And cast the unprofitable servant into the outer darkness. There will be weeping

and gnashing of teeth." Matthew 25:14-30, NKJV.

I just want to mention why Jesus used the word 'Talents' in His parable. Usually, it's described as a huge "Sum of Money."

CHAPTER THREE

Parables in the Book of Mark

Pharisees Questioned About Fasting: These Pharisees had many questions about fasting. These religious members were fasting; they realized that the disciples of Jesus did not fast. So, they questioned Jesus: We fast, but your followers are not fasting. Jesus answered: while the bridegroom is with them, they will not fast now. But the time comes, the bridegroom will be taken away from them they will fast later.

"As long as they have the bridegroom with them, they cannot fast. But the days will come when the bridegroom will be taken away from

them, and then they will fast in those days."

them, and then they will fast in those days."
Mark 2:18-20, NKJV.

Kingdom Divided Cannot Stand: There is a
parable we can learn from Jesus' teaching. Jesus
began casting out an evil spirit out of people's
life. Everyone who was there, especially His own
family and Pharisees accused Him that Jesus has
Beelzebub. He was casting out demons by the
ruler of Satan. Jesus called his disciples to himself: How can demons cast out devils? If a Kingdom divided cannot stand.

If Satan is coming against itself, he cannot
stand that would be the end. He said: a house divided cannot stand also. If someone is trying to
attack a strong man in his house without tying
him up, then he can rob the persons' home.

**"If a kingdom is divided against itself, that
kingdom cannot stand. And if a house is divided against itself, that house cannot stand."**
Mark 3:23-27, NKJV.

Light Under a Basket: The Word is the Light
in our spirit, soul, and body. We can use the
Light so that we can see the beautiful things of
God in our spiritual walk with Jesus. When we
have the Word in our hearts, and the Holy Spirit

will show us where we need to go. If we set our light under a basket and cover it, then no one can see how God has done great work in our lives.

Jesus said: Put your light on a lampstand that everyone can see what the Lord has made miracles and healing in your life. There is no need to hide your Christian life and let your light shine. Let every man will recognize the Glory of God; they may see Jesus through your life. One lost soul can receive Jesus for eternity.

He said: Is everyone who has an ear, let him hear my word. Those who hear the word and obey the Word of God will be given more. If anyone who thinks they have everything but not obey the Word, what they have, it will be taken away from them.

"For whoever has, to him more will be given; but whoever does not have, even what he has will be taken away from him." Mark 4:21-25, NKJV.

The Growing Seed: This parable would connect with growing seed. It relates the Kingdom of God to a fellow man who spreads seed on the ground in his field. The man goes to rest and sleep, and he does his own business, went on his workday by day. He doesn't know how the seed grows from the ground. The seed affects, and the seed will grow. Thus, it makes a stalk and leaves, then ahead of wheat or any crop used as food. The matter is the plant develops without the farmer's interference.

Probably no one can understand how nature functions without our intentions. A man just planted his seed on the ground with good soil. Nature works on its own, with no one's help or anyone's assistant. The seed grows to sprout. The earth does all the work of seed and grows crops by itself. When the first blade comes out, and the head shows up, that we know the full grain is ready.

We see the grain ripens; the time of harvest is near. They began to put in the sickle, reap crops with a good harvest. It processes that God can perform His purposes, indeed when we are away or unaware of what He's making. Then, and eventually, it's quite getting formed grains in the head. It is with no man's help or any man's knowledge. Growing seed under the soil and the man will know the time of harvest is near.

Nature will bring forth a result of the seed to harvest. The fact is, God accomplishes His Word in the life of an individual, which is mysterious through human effort. May we be steadfast in sowing the seed which is the Word of God, asking for harvest, and allowing the Lord will bring a great result.

Jesus is saying: the seed is the Word that will plant in the heart of every person. No one can know how the Lord works in the heart of every man. The heart of a man is like "The earth or the ground" The ground will respond to the message of God's Word. It will grow, the man will open his heart to God, and to receive God's love and Grace. Who would give water the seed on the ground? The spirit of God does it! The harvest will come by God's mercy toward man's life.

"For the earth yields crops by itself: first the blade, then the head, after that the full grain in the head. But when the grain ripens, immediately he puts in the sickle, because the harvest has come." Mark 4:26-29, NKJV.

The Mustard Seed: We read another parable about a mustard seed: Jesus said: A mustard seed is like the Kingdom of heaven; A man sowed a seed in his field. A mustard seed is the smallest seed in all other grains in the world. When a seed started to grow in good soil and making a root, then to become mighty. So, this seed planted and turned into a tree better than herbs. The birds of the air made to nest in its branches.

It means: the seed can be the Word and the Gospel; The man is Jesus. The field represents the world that hears the Word and receives Jesus as Lord and Savior. So, the tree began to have a firm root in Jesus. The birds of the air represent: When the tree is growing to make a shade for God's people and making a refuge for faithful believers. The tree is also making a resting place for birds.

"but when it is sown, it grows up and becomes greater than all herbs, and shoots out large branches, so that the birds of the air may nest under its shade." Mark 4:30-32, NKJV.

The Transfiguration of Jesus: There will be a complete transformation with Jesus' appearance into Glory that turned out like into the light. Transfiguration of Jesus mentioned in the New Testament became shined in triumph up the mountain. After six days later, the Word said: Jesus took Peter, James, and John up a mountain to pray.

Suddenly Jesus has transformed with new clothes shining, utterly white with Glory. There was no way to find any clothes on the earth can be compared with Jesus' clothes. Jesus's disciples saw Elijah and Moses have appeared talking to Jesus. They were all watching; then Peter went to Jesus said to Him, Rabbi, let's make three tabernacles: one for you, one for Elijah, one for Moses.

The Glory of the Lord came upon them: they heard, the voice in the middle of clouds saying: This is my Son, listen to Him! They looked around; they didn't see anyone except Jesus standing by Himself alone. They all came down from Mountain with Jesus. He commanded them not to tell anyone else about this event but after His resurrection!

Jesus mentioned to disciples that the Son of Man must die and rise again. They asked Him: Why Ellijay would come first? He said: Elijah must come; he restores everything. But the Son of Man must suffer, and they will not believe in Him, will be rejected.

"Then He answered and told them, "Indeed, Elijah is coming first and restores all things. And how is it written concerning the Son of Man, that He must suffer many things and be treated with contempt?" Mark 9:1-13, NKJV.

Tasteless Salt Is Worthless: Our ways of life can have a good or a bad impact on people around us. As we know, every man is striving to become perfect in life. But Jesus has further instructed us to focus on the internal which sin can affect our hearts. Jesus chooses us to be salt, carrying the sweetness message of God into the evil environment. We realize that all salt applied in fertilizers.

How can anyone transform into salt? Salt is an effect used to preserve foodstuffs, using for meat. Salt uses to kill viruses or germ developing. Then, in this matter, Jesus said, salt in Christians believers can block the increase of sin. So, there is generally known the purpose of salt. We can stay away from our sinful human desire, and we can focus on making ourselves clean from all unrighteousness. So, we have to become a model for everyone, not by receiving such immoral action.

"For everyone will be seasoned with fire, and every sacrifice will be seasoned with salt. Salt is good, but if the salt loses its flavor, how will you season it? Have salt in yourselves, and have peace with one another." Mark 9:49-50, NKJV.

Jesus Blessed the Children: Many people were coming to Jesus and bringing their children to touch Him. Disciples of Jesus rebuked them not to touch Jesus. But Jesus saw them the children were trying to come near to Him, and He was very displeased. He said: Let these little children come to me, do not hinder them; the kingdom of God belongs to them as well.

He said: if anyone does not accept the kingdom of God like a little child, it will not be able to enter. Then Jesus took all of them into His arms. He laid His hands on them, love them, and blessed them.

"Assuredly, I say to you, whoever does not receive the kingdom of God as a little child will by no means enter it. And He took them up in His arms, laid His hands on them, and blessed them." Mark 10:13-16, NKJV.

Becoming a Servant to Serve: As we read about Jesus's disciples, they came and asked Him to receive a petition from Him. They said we have a request and we want you to give us our petition. Later Jesus said; I will, what do you want from me? Please grant us that one would sit at your right hand, and the other one would sit on the left side in Your glory. Jesus makes very clear instruction to His disciples, for those who had thought to become an important person in His kingdom.

His disciples thought, if they may find a place sitting at the right or left-hand side of Jesus, they may become great in life. But Jesus had prepared a better ministry for them to carry the message of the Kingdom of God.

In this statement, Jesus describes to His disciples. He had to correct their ambition with kindness and humility, not undermining any possible disagreements among the twelve disciples. But instead, Jesus didn't blame James and John for wishing to become great.

At the same time, He prepares them for the great outpouring of the Holy Spirit. He will show them what greatness actually means and how to carry out the message of hope and preaching the Good News to the entire world. A passion for greatness must be a sacrificial ministry. God has called us to be strong in spirit and to accomplish marvelous works.

The Lord chooses us to have a goal to focus on Him. He cherishes to prepare us that we yearn to serve God and others. To have a serving heart is making us great in the Kingdom. Serving the only One who is glorious in the highest above all names. But I believe true greatness would have taken place with a cost in which Jesus gave Himself with a high price on the cross for us.

We find the power of His love as we walk along with Him that He prepares us receiving a pure servanthood's heart. Jesus is reminding us in His Word: I came to serve, but not to be served. We find greatness in serving.

"And whoever of you desires to be first shall be slave of all. For even the Son of Man did not come to be served, but to serve, and to give His life a ransom for many." Mark 10:35-45, NKJV.

Beware of the Scribes: We learn about the scribes in ancient Israel, these men who were interested in studying the Law, they interpret it, and to rewrite comments on it. Jesus began to rebuke the scribes for their dishonesty and their hypocrisy. They studied the Law, and they trained others, but they did not want to obey God. The scribes' initial purpose was to recognize and to keep the Law. They needed to encourage others to carry on.

They were an ancient Jewish record-keeper; they taught the people about the Law. The public generally admired them because of their intellect, commitment, and good character in Law-keeping.

Jesus predicted His disciples to be cautious of the scribes. He said: these men who have a motive to go around the town and showing off with long robes. They are trying to greet people with shaking hands in marketplaces with their love, but they have no kindness in their hearts. They are seeking to sit in the best place in the synagogues. When they go to attend the feast, they like to sit in the most beautiful area. When these men who will visit other widow's houses to devour all food. If they are doing good for others but are pretending with a long prayer, these men will have greater condemnation.

It's a good lesson for every Christian believer in studying from the deceitfulness of the scribes. God requires us to seek Him to higher praise of holiness inside-out. He demands an internal transformation of spirit that is continually submitting in His passion and obedience to the Lord Jesus.

"Then He said to them in His teaching, "Beware of the scribes, who desire to go around in long robes, love greetings in the marketplaces, the best seats in the synagogues, and the best places at feasts, who devour widows' houses, and for a pretense make long prayers. These

will receive greater condemnation." Mark 12:38-40, NKJV.

Poor Widow Offering: Jesus and His disciples were sitting in front of the temple treasury. They were watching the people, how they give their money into the treasury. Jesus saw many rich people were coming and putting their money out of their richness. He noticed that there is one poor widow came to offer her money, but she had only small copper coins dropping into the treasury.

Jesus called all of His disciples to himself. He said to them: This widow was dropping small copper coins out of her poverty, not having any penny to live. But those rich people entered into the temple and dropping their money out of their wealth. God loves cheerful givers, whatever is a small amount giving to the Kingdom of God. He accepts it, and it will be given back to us with a great reward. God is the God of the giver, and He is our provision's God.

"Assuredly, I say to you that this poor widow has put in more than all those who have given to the treasury; 44 for they all put in out of their abundance, but she out of her poverty put

in all that she had, her whole livelihood." Mark 12:41-44, NKJV.

The Fig Tree: Jesus will teach us through this beautiful parable the fig tree, which is about His return. Jesus said: when you see the tree is mild and leaves come out, then you recognize that the summer is near to us. Nature will give us an understanding of the work of God. He created everything for His own glory and His pleasure. Jesus describes that His return is near, and He is standing right at the door. This generation will not pass away unless to see these things taken place. He said: I tell you, heaven and earth will pass away, but My Word will never pass away!

"Assuredly, I say to you, this generation will by no means pass away till all these things take place. Heaven and earth will pass away, but My words will by no means pass away" Mark 13:28-31, NKJV.

CHAPTER FOUR

Parables in the Book of Luke

New **Wine into New Wineskins:** We recognize in this parable reveals to us about; do not put new wine in an old wineskin. In fact, new wine demands a new wineskin because as a new wine increases during the fermentation will be transformed, and it will expand the wineskin. An old wineskin will break under the force of new wine. But we put new wine into new wineskins, and both are protected.

Jesus emphasizes the life we have in Him. It means that we can't compromise traditional religious practices with a new faith in Jesus. Therefore, there will be no need to pursue the ritual self-righteous formalities. We must follow Jesus only and not living in our own acting-based spirituality.

"But new wine must be put into new wineskins, and both are preserved." Luke 5:37-39, NKJV.

The Beatitudes: The term Beatitude appears with a definition: "blessedness." The words mean: 'blessed are' in each message of beatitude involves an expression of happiness or prosperity. This statement had a compelling interest in "spiritual comfort and true joy" to the people. Jesus was speaking with gladness and delight to those who have these sweet characters inside of their lives. While He was told of the present time "blessedness," He encouraged an excellent award for the future.

Many translations and instructions presented about the beatitudes through the facts revealed. Most commentators acknowledged that the beatitudes show us a way of life in God.

The word "poor in spirit," says the acknowledgment of something regarding spiritual suffering or poverty. It specifies someone who sees his desire looking for God. Jesus used this phrase:

"The kingdom of heaven," it relates to the king as God and people who accept Him as the ruler of heaven. **"Blessed are you poor, For yours is the kingdom of God."** Luke 6:20.

The Word is "Hunger" would have the meaning of a profound desire of the human spirit and is needed an inspiring Word of God. The Lord will fill up a hungriness of those who are looking to be filled with His Word. He is overflowing empty and thirst hearts with the joy of the Lord. **"Blessed are you who hunger now, For you shall be filled."** Luke 6:21a.

The Word said those who wept and had a long-suffering in the past. If there was a sin caused us to suffer in life. We repent over it, and God is a wonderful God. It is time to rejoice in the salvation of God. We are blessed now, for us to laugh and be glad in it. **"Blessed are you who weep now, For you shall laugh."** Luke 6:21b.

Jesus encouraged us to have a mindset to move forward in this life which any man hates us or reject us. Even though we want to be a witness of the Lord, but they refuse the Word of God. As we know, Jesus is with us, who can be against us. We rejoice in Him in whom we have the Life of

Christ, not trust any man. So, Jesus said we are blessed because of Him who is higher than anything else in the world. **"Blessed are you when men hate you, And when they exclude you."** Luke 6:22a.

Jesus says if anyone who criticizes you or deny you because of Me. But if they will deny you, they will reject Me. If they accuse you with a false witness as evil for the sake of the Son of Man. So, we can remember that we are not alone. He is surrounding us with all His Goodness. We declare that we are living in victory in the Lord Jesus. **"And revile you, and cast out your name as evil, For the Son of Man's sake."** Luke 6:22b.

The Lord will tell us to rejoice the day of the Lord, and when the time will come to see Him face to face. Nothing can be lost, but our labor is going to be rewarded by Him. He knows how we have served God and served others. How we have helped those who couldn't help themselves. He rewards us because He loves us. Let's do our duty as a child and a servant. We will be a good servant in His Kingdom. He said: Your reward will be greater in heaven. He has already prepared us for eternal life, and we are ready to meet

Him soon. **"Rejoice in that day and leap for joy! For indeed your reward is great in heaven, For in like manner their fathers did to the prophets."** Luke 6:23. NKJV.

Can the Blind Lead the Blind: Jesus will give a powerful illustration of a blind man. Is it possible a blind man leads another blind man? Do you think they are leading each other in the right direction? No, it will be both falls down into a ditch. Jesus mentioned here: why do you see a speck in your brother's eyes, you're a hypocrite! You do not see any speck in your own eyes first. How can you help someone else, but you are still judging your brother from your heart. You are accusing him that he is not righteous before God, but you are making spiritually blind eyes for yourself. At the same time, you are trying to save others? How can you save yourself?

He goes on saying: Look at your own eyes, if there is a sin of pride in your life, remove it first. Then you will be free from your sins. Then you see God better for yourself then you live with a righteous heart. A follower of Jesus is not above His master, but everyone is hungry to learn about Jesus and to become a disciple of Him.

"And He spoke a parable to them: "Can the blind lead the blind? Will they, not both fall into the ditch?" Luke 6:39-42, NKJV.

Sitting and Complaining in the Marketplace: Jesus wondered why these Pharisees and those lawmakers had rejected the will of God, and these people deny the truth of God for themselves. They heard the message from John Baptist and did not get water baptism by him either.

Jesus responded: what can I say about these men? What then can I compare that you will always complain to your friends? When you sit in the marketplace and talking with all your friends. Jesus gave a sample; if we play the flute for you, you don't like it. If we mourned for you, you still dislike it, and you do not even want to weep. How can we satisfy you? You are a complaint generation, not to be grateful.

"They are like children sitting in the marketplace and calling to one another" Luke 7:31-32, NKJV.

Moneylender had Two Debtors: Jesus was sharing about a moneylender who had two debtors. These two owed money; one owed five hundred denarii and the other one who owed fifty.

They came to him and said: we have no money to pay you back. So, what moneylender did, he forgave them, and let them go. There were free of their debts. Jesus asked His disciples: which one of these two debtors love him more? One of the disciples, Simon, said: the one who had debt and forgave more. Jesus said: You are saying the right thing. It means: No matter how many sins we have committed, big sins, and small sins.

When we come to the presence of Jesus, He is able to forgive all of our sins. When we repent our mistakes, He can remove all our rebellion, pride, and bad habit. It's evident that these two debtors owed money to the moneylender. They came to him, asked him, and we have no money to pay you back. We see he forgave them all their debtors. The Lord can do whenever we are ready to accept His forgiveness.

"And when they had nothing with which to repay, he freely forgave them both. Tell Me, therefore, which of them will love him more?" Luke 7:41-43, NKJV.

A Samaritan Village Rejects Jesus: We will look at three specific groups of people in this situation: Jesus was leaving toward Jerusalem. Jesus passed by Samaritan Village with the people's rejection of hearts toward Jesus. James & John's disciples were walking along with their Teacher. We learn that Jesus's assignment was very important than anything else for Him. He wanted to move on to finish the course of His mission what the Father has given Him to accomplish. No matter the Samaritan people in their village rejected His coming. But He passed by and went to the next town and to preach and teach the Eternal Word of God.

Sometimes we need to think about what our intention is to figure out, its associates whether our own purposes with Jesus's mission. We are usually concentrating on our own plan, but we do neglect Jesus's mission. That's why Jesus taught us how to seek His Kingdom first. The people of Samaritan village acknowledged Jesus' persistence to go to Jerusalem. So, they made their decision not to serve Jesus. Even they did not want to make all His arrangements for him on his journey and along with His disciples to stay with them.

We learn from His disciples James and John how they reacted to these people of Village. I also believe these two disciples were offended; we see in this verse said: James and John said to Jesus. Lord, if you want us to command, the fire of God come down from heaven to consume them just like Elijah did. These two disciples were furious and tried to convince Jesus to wipe out the entire village because people have not welcomed them.

Still, Jesus loves them, He rebukes James and John said to them. I came to save a man's lives but not to destroy them. No matter these people have denied Jesus, but He loves them unconditionally. This is the love of the Father who has sent His only begotten Son to save the entire world, not perish but to have everlasting life.

"But He turned and rebuked them, and said, "You do not know what manner of spirit you are of. For the Son of Man did not come to destroy men's lives but to save them." And they went to another village." Luke 9:51-56, NKJV.

Dead Bury Their Own Dead, Follow Me: The time came that some followers became a follower of Jesus and some had an excuse not follow Him or not to serve God. They were there with Jesus and learning how to grow into a servant of God. But their life had not allowed them fully to follow and to become a servant God. They gave a straightforward excuse not to follow Him. Jesus called one of the followers into His Kingdom, and He said: Follow Me. He answered to Jesus, let me go to bury my father, then I come back to follow you and serve you. Jesus responded to him: You may allow the dead to bury the dead, but you will follow me and go to preach the Kingdom of God.

"Then He said to another, "Follow Me." But he said, "Lord, let me first go and bury my father." Jesus said to him, "Let the dead bury their own dead, but you go and preach the kingdom of God." Luke 9:59-60, NKJV.

A Cost to Follow Him: Jesus had a journey on the road, there was a man came to Him; Tell Him; Jesus, I will follow You wherever you go! Jesus answered him: you may see foxes will have holes, and birds have nests, even so, the Son of Man does not have any place to go or to lay His head. There is a cost to follow Jesus. If someone will follow Jesus, he needs to leave everything behind in this world, to become a disciple of Jesus.

We can accept Him as Lord and Savior, and then a new life of Jesus will penetrate in our old life. We become a new creation in Christ. He will come into our lives by His Holy Spirit, and we live in righteous life in the Lord Jesus.

"Jesus said to him, "Foxes have holes and birds of the air have nests, but the Son of Man

has nowhere to lay His head." Luke 9:57-58, NKJV.

Woe to the Impenitent Cities: Jesus spoke about these impenitent cities, Woe to them. As we search to know about these two ancient villages of Chorazin and Bethsaida were located in Israel. These two cities were far from Capernaum.

Tyre and Sidon, these two Gentile cities also were heathen and located on the seashore of the Mediterranean. As it appears that Jesus has not ever passed through, he was usually a short distance away from them. The explanation is about Tyre and Sidon, and they would have confessed their sins to the God of Israel with the confession of serious repentance in the past. But, they didn't, it would have seen their guilt and confusion to change from their an immoral act. Also, Jesus did not go to heathen cities if He went, they would have accepted Him better than the Jews cities.

Sackcloth was a rough cloth from camel's hair, or goat hair was putting on who had grieved. They figured it out sackcloth because being hard and stable. They needed it for carrying out the giant sacks in which they made rough features on the backs of camels. Ashes were putting upon the head and face as other types of sorrow. Jesus here expresses these significant remarks to show that these cities would have repented a long time ago.

Jesus said, when you speak my Word, he who hears the Word if he will reject it, reject me, not you. He rejects Me, rejects Him who has sent Me. **"He who hears you hears Me, he who rejects you rejects Me, and he who rejects Me rejects Him who sent Me."** Luke 10:13-16, NKJV.

Good Samaritan had Compassion: There was a certain expert lawyer who wanted to tempt Jesus. He came to Him, asking a question: Teacher, what can I do to gain eternal life? Jesus answered: what you were told in the law? He replied: **"So he answered and said, 'You shall love the Lord your God with all your heart, with all your soul, with all your strength, and with all your mind,' and 'your neighbor as yourself.'"** Luke 10:27, NKJV. He wanted to defend himself, and he asked Jesus again: Who is my neighbor? Jesus gave a good story that the man would understand who his neighbor is?

Jesus continues saying about Good Samaritan: There was a man who had a journey from Jerusalem to Jericho. The thieves have attacked him, and they robbed him. They took all his belonging and wounded him on the way. They left him on the sideroad half dead. Some people came around and saw him, but they had no pay attention to him. A priest came along, and he looked at the half-dead man on the road. He also saw him; He went on his way. Another a Levite man came, saw him, at the same he didn't have any kindness to a wounded man who laid down half dead.

Finally, a Samaritan man passed by, he saw him; He had compassion on him. He went to him; he bandaged his wounds; he took his oil and wine for taking care of him. He sat him on his own animal, took him to an inn that he will get rest to recover from his wounds. He stayed there with him until the next day, before he leaves the inn, he told the innkeeper to watch over the wounded man. He will be paying innkeeper when he comes his way back and repaying more.

Jesus asked him: which one of three persons can be his neighbor that the thieves hurt him? He answered Jesus: The one who had mercy on him, Jesus said: Go, also do to others.

"But a certain Samaritan, as he journeyed, came where he was. And when he saw him, he had compassion." Luke 10:25-37, NKJV.

Mary and Martha Served Jesus: Jesus and his disciples were coming down to a village. There were two sisters, Mary and Martha, who heard about the coming of Jesus, they went to meet Him, invited Him to stay in their home. They came in the house, Jesus began to teach the Word of God, Mary was sitting in the front of Jesus listing to His teaching. Probably they were many guests invited along with Jesus and His disciples welcomed in their home too.

Martha was very busy preparing food and organizing everything which it would be honorable to serve Jesus as their guests. Martha needed help, so; she went to find Mary; she saw Mary sitting down and listing to the teaching of Jesus. Martha said, Lord, I am trying to prepare everything to serve you, and serve other guests, tell Mary to come and help me. Jesus said: Martha, Martha; you are worried and troubled about many events. But when Mary was sitting and listing to the Word of God, Mary has chosen an excellent thing, and it cannot take away from her.

Mary has chosen to sit down in Jesus' presence and listen to the Word of the Lord because the Word is Jesus and Life. We get swamped in this life; we remind ourselves that we can come into God's presence. He brings us joy and peace to fulfill our lives.

"And Jesus answered and said to her, "Martha, Martha, you are worried and troubled about many things. But one thing is needed, and Mary has chosen that good part, which will not be taken away from her." Luke 10:38-42, NKJV.

A Friend With Unexpecting Visit: Jesus said: A man was sleeping with his family in his house at night. His friend came to knock at his door in the middle of the night. His friend said, I got an unexpected visit, which he arrived from a far journey. I have no food or bread to offer to my quest. So, he asks him, can I lend three loads of bread, I just received a visit tonight. His friend even didn't open the door for him. He said behind the door: I am sleeping with my family, and my children are getting rest. I cannot rise to give it to you, and the door already closed.

Jesus said: I tell you the truth, because of his persistent, he will get up from his bed, he will give him what he needs to provide food for his quest. When we cry out to Him, and our persistent prayer provides us with the assurance that God hears our prayer.

"I say to you, though he will not rise and give to him because he is his friend, yet because of his persistence he will rise and give him as many as he needs." Luke 11:5-8, NKJV.

Keeping the Word: When Jesus was preaching and teaching the Word of God, there was a woman from the crowd who raised her voice saying. She said, **"Blessed is the womb that bore You, and the breasts which nursed You!"**

There is an authoritative answer we hear from Jesus to the woman and all crowded people. I believe Jesus is the Word, and He came to bring Life to sinful man. The Word is Jesus, who speaks the truth to any man who has not heard the Good News of Jesus. He mentioned: You hear the Word and obey the Word, Jesus said: 'you are blessed.'

Jesus wants us to take-in the Word God by faith, and believe His Word; it brings New Life into spirit, soul, mind, and body. He came to bring salvation to our sinful world. He gave His life, and He crucified for our sins and sickness. He died and rose again. He is alive today. Jesus said:

"More than that, blessed are those who hear the word of God and keep it!" Luke 11:27-28, NKJV.

The Lamp of your Body: Jesus mentioned here: if someone has lit a lamp. No one can turn it on in a secret place or put it under a basket. But when we set a lampstand up and those who will enter and see the light. Jesus said the lamp is the eyes of your body. When the eyes are good, you will see the light, when your eyes are bad, you will see the darkness in your body. Jesus said: When your spiritual life will come into the light of God, the whole soul and body and spirit become full of the light of God.

We desire God to recognize Him in our spiritual eyes if we become hungry for His Words. He is going to visit us in a powerful way. When we sin against God, we see darkness. Let's allow Him to make a new life for us by His Grace and Mercy. He will make us His light shins on us, and He makes us a bright future in Him. If we know the sins will bring darkness in our spirit, then we cannot see the Glory of God. We repent and ask Him to forgive all of our sins. He makes new things again, and He gives us a new spiritual eye to see better.

"If then your whole body is full of light, having no part dark, the whole body will be full of light, as when the bright shining of a lamp gives you light." Luke 11:33-36, NKJV.

Jesus Teaches the Fear of God: Let's study what the Lord Jesus teaches us to have a fear of God. He inspires us not to be frightened of those who are trying to kill the body, what they can do more to us. But they cannot kill your spirit. He said: I will show you how you would have a fear of God in your heart to whom you should give respect and honor. The One who has all power and Glory to cast them out and those who go to hell.

Fear God the One who is worthy to all praise in heaven and earth. Jesus will say to us; we are precious in God's eyes. He will never leave behind by ourselves. He is always watching over us. When we turn over our lives into His authority, we belong to Him. We received Him by faith; we believe He is covering us by His presence.

There is a powerful illustration of protection. He said God knows about every area of our lives even He knows the numbers of our hairs. Because we are a valuable child to Him, He loves us.

"But the very hairs of your head are all numbered. Do not fear therefore; you are of more value than many sparrows." Luke 12:4-7, NKJV.

The Rich Fool Man: There was a rich man who had a farm that produces good crops. He had many good harvests every year, his barns were small and became full even to overflowing of grain. He said to himself: I have too much harvest of my crops. I need to have big barns to keep them, what I want to do! I will tear down the small barn, building a big barn for all the crops. Then I will sit back, and I have plenty of crops, and my barn will be filled with the harvest.

I will enjoy myself with wine, with a woman, sing a good song. I will get relaxed for the rest of my life. So, when God would say to you: You are a fool! Tonight you are going to die, who will get all of your possession? Jesus said: every person can expect, this is the way to enjoy life and become rich temporarily in this world. But you will not get rich in heaven.

"But God said to him, Fool! This night your soul will be required of you; then whose will those things be which you have provided? So is he who lays up treasure for himself, and is not rich toward God." Luke 12:16-21, NKJV.

The Faithful Servant and the Evil Servant: Here, what the Lord warned His disciples, and His faithful servants, to make them ready for His return. As we are servants of Jesus, He called us to set our focuses, souls, mind, and our hearts on the Kingdom of God. He encouraged us to refuse any lust of the flesh and not having earthly desires in the world. We would have the experience that to set our treasure and inheritance up in heaven. We are called to serve the Lord, to honor Him, to follow Him, and to glorify Him. He told us to wait on Him, and we stand watchful of His return, and to receive Him in the Rapture.

He revealed to His servants to what actually occurs in the forthcoming of His appearing and will happen on the hour as expected. He is recommending them to continue to be attentive. He said; you would never be surprised at all seasons; warning His servants to be active in the ministry. His Return is at any moment, which will be as sudden as happened to a thief at midnight.

The Lord spoke of some vital topic to His unfaithful and untrustworthy servants whom He considered them as evil and unstable in life, not serving and caring for others. Their behavior and attitude make them a severe punishment. These unfaithful servants should be supposed to encourage God's people being thankful for the Grace and mercy of God. They must stand in the gap as an intercessor to watch the people of God for their spiritual life. But they have grown into instead an inspiration to Satan and opens up themselves to be controlled by the devil.

"But know this, that if the master of the house had known what hour the thief would come, he would have watched and not allowed his house to be broken into. Therefore you also be ready, for the Son of Man is coming at an hour you do not expect." Luke 12:35-40, NKJV.

Repent or Perish: The Lord Jesus is telling us in this verse; there are two chooses, 'repent or perish.' Which one would we have to choose? We know that Jesus came for all sinners, and there is none righteous before God. The Word said, 'we all have sinned, come short the glory of God.' So, because God has been gracious to us. He does not want us to live without Him, and there will not be any destiny for us. When we hear the Good News of Jesus, which is He made sacrificed on the cross for us. We should suppose to pay our own penalty, and Jesus was willing to go on the cross by the plan of the Father in heaven.

He already paid the price for all. We will not need to pay the penalty of sins for ourselves. It's finished, Jesus has won the victory. Salvation is available for every man who believes in his heart and accepts Jesus as Lord and Savior.

"I tell you, no; but unless you repent you will all likewise perish." Luke 13:1-5, NKJV.

A Barren Fig Tree with no Fruit: There was a man who owned a vineyard who plants a fig tree for three years. The time of harvest, he went to see if there is a fruit on the fig tree. But he could find none, and he asked his vineyard keeper; lets cut this fig tree down, it doesn't bear any fruit? We will use this fig tree ground for another fruit tree better. The vineyard keeper answered him, leave it alone, let me dig around the tree and fertilize it.

It may be helpful if it does not give any fruit next year. Then we cut the tree down. The perfect illustration that God is trying to help us to have a good fruit of life. He is trying to strengthen our faith to believe in His promise. He will give a second chance if we don't follow God's way. Then we cut down our blessing by our own choice from Him; there will not be any fruit in Christian life.

"Sir, let it alone this year also until I dig around it and fertilize it. And if it bears fruit, well. But if not, after that you can cut it down." Luke 13:6-9, NKJV.

Humble Themselves, be Exalted: Jesus gave an excellent illustration about placing yourself in high place by yourself. Jesus gave a story about if someone has invited you for a wedding feast. When you arrived there, do not sit in the high honor place before the host asked too. It might be they have invited other honorable guests, and the host will place them wherever they want their guests to sit.

If you sit in a high place, the host will ask you to go to the lowest place to sit; that would be humiliating! When you arrived at the wedding feast, sitting in the lowest place first. Later the host of the house will come to you and welcome you to sit next to honorable people. Jesus continues saying: If anyone exalts himself shall be humbled, but someone who humbles himself will be exalted.

"For all those who exalt themselves will be humbled, and those who humble themselves will be exalted." Luke 14:7-11, NKJV.

Leaving All to Follow Christ: There was a great multitude followed by Jesus. He said to them; if anyone decides to follow me, he does not hate his father, mother, wife, children, sisters, and brothers. Not even hate his own life, he cannot be My disciple. He continued saying, if he cannot carry his cross daily and follow me with all his heart, he cannot be My disciple. I think Jesus tells us about leaving everything in the world behind.

Recognize our weaknesses and our sinful attitudes. If we cannot cleanse ourselves in our own way, let us Jesus will do for us, if we allow Him to come into our lives. He will come to remove our sins, and He cleanses our spirit. He makes a new person; then we can rejoice in His blessings. Then the Holy Spirit comes into the clean life by our repentance, and we invite Jesus as the Son of God. We confess Jesus as the Savior and Lord. Amen.

"And whoever does not bear his cross and come after Me cannot be My disciple." Luke 14:25-27, NKJV.

Cost of Discipleship: For which of you, wishing to establish a tower, first, he will make his mind and how to make a wisely plan to build.

It would be an excellent thought to settle down to calculate the cost, whether he has sufficient resources to finish it? Otherwise, when he prepared a ground base and but he is not capable of completing the task. If everyone who observes him, saying, this fellow started to build the tower, and he was not capable of accomplishing it.

Jesus shared another one: there is a king who will go out to war to confront another king. Do you think the king will not lay down his plan of strike first and consult whether he is capable of ten thousand who goes against him with twenty thousand? And if not, while the other king is also thinking a good withdrawal from the war. He appoints a messenger to be sent and pleads for a proposal of peace. So then, is any man is not willing to come after me and deny himself, it cannot be my disciples.

"So likewise, whoever of you does not forsake all that he has cannot be My disciple. " Luke 14:28-33, NKJV.

The Lost Coin: There is a great illustration that can reveal here: A woman had ten coins, which she lost them all. The woman tried to find them, but there was no way she could find them. She goes to light a lamp; probably, she adds more oil into it and to search for the lost coins. She cleans the house, sweeps the floor. She was really trying to find these coins. Finally, she finds her lost coins; she went to her friends and neighbors around to tell them: I found my ten lost coins; come and rejoice with me.

It means: many souls have lost when one soul can be found. There will be a great joy in heaven, and rejoicing in the presence of God over one soul has repented his sin and coming back into the Kingdom of God.

"Likewise, I say to you, there is joy in the presence of the angels of God over one sinner who repents" Luke 15:8-10, NKJV.

The Lost Son Alive again: There was a man who had two sons, the youngest son came to his father said: Father, would you give my inheritance which belongs to me. So, the father divided the entire estate between two sons. The younger son took all his possessions from his father. He took off to a far country; he went to make a journey by himself wherever he wants to do with his life? After a while, the younger son spending all his possessions; he came to nothing.

The Word said: there was a famine in the country, where the younger son stayed over that land. He tried to make his life in the right direction to survive in a foreign land. He went to work, and they sent him to work to taking care of swine. Because of the famine, there was no food can be found. No one gave him anything to eat. He was there with the pigs; he began to eat pods the swine ate. He started to think, why am I doing here? Famine is approaching the land; I have spent all my money, nothing left for me to live.

Finally, he came to himself: I will go back to my father's house. I will ask him that I can work for him as a servant; at least it will better than here. I will not perish with hunger. I will tell my father; I have sinned against you and heaven. I cannot be called your son anymore; I am not worthy of being called your son. I will be like one of your servants to work.

Then he rose and went to his father's house. His father knew that his younger son would be coming back home soon. The father was standing on the roadway and waiting for his son to come back home. When the father saw his son is coming toward him, the father ran to him, kiss, and hug him, welcome him back home.

The son said to his father: I have sinned against you and heaven. I will no longer be called your son, but let me be your servant to work for you. But the father said to his servant: bring the best robe putting on him, bring a ring to put on his hand, bring sandals for his feet. The father was delighted to meet his son. He said: bring the fatted calf, kill it, let's rejoice and eat all together. Because my son was lost, but now he found, and he is alive again.

At the same time, the older brother came after a long day's work, and he walked near to the house. He heard there was sound music, laughing and rejoicing in the house. He called one of the servants to find out what is going on? The servant said: your brother came home safe and alive again. The older brother became very angry, and he didn't want to go inside the house.

His father came out of the house; he was happy to see him, tell his older brother about his younger brother came home safely. The older brother said to his father: I have been with you all these years. I have severed you and worked hard, but you never gave anything to make time off to enjoy with my friends. But your younger son came back home, he lost all his money, and nothing left for himself. You will still have welcomed him.

The father said you are always with me. Let's rejoice together because your younger brother was lost. Now he is alive and living with us again. Our Father is still welcoming and celebrating our coming back home.

"for this my son was dead and is alive again; he was lost and is found. And they began to be merry." Luke 15:11-31, NKJV.

Unjust Steward Manager: Jesus shared about a shrewd manager to His disciples. There was a rich man who has given authority over his manager to taking care of his possessions. He heard about his manager that he is not managing well. He called in; he asked him: are you not interested any longer in managing my possessions?

The manager thought that the owner might be taking his job away from him. He needs to do something about before he will be out of work. He said to himself; I cannot work hard enough; if I lose my job, at least I will be welcomed into other people's homes. Later on, I will not lose my respect or reputation.

He said to himself, what I am going to do now. I am calling every person who owes money to my master, and I will make a deal with them. So, he called to one who owed money: he asked him: how much money do you owe; he said: nine hundred gallons of olive oil; You may pay four hundred and fifty. Another man came who owed money, and he asked him: How much money do you owe: a thousand bushels of wheat; you may pay eight hundred.

He reduced the debt amount of his friends to those who owe money to his master. He realized he might be losing his job, later on, to make many worldly friends welcome him again. The manager decided to make his master happy with deceitful hearts but making his friends glad about a dishonest act. So, then the master who found out that the manager was very misleading his work, and he acted shrewdly with an unjust steward manager. Because of having a wrong thought, it may lose all God's blessing.

Jesus said: You may make a friend for yourself with unlawful money; if you fail, they will not receive you always with an everlasting home. Be faithful and, it will be given to you many more blessings. Jesus said: No person; not anyone can serve two masters, 'money' or 'God?'

"No servant can serve two masters; for either he will hate the one and love the other, or else he will be loyal to the one and despise the other. You cannot serve God and mammon." Luke 16:1-13, NKJV.

The Law, the Prophets, and the Kingdom:
Now the Pharisees who knew that Jesus taught
the Word. They were greedy and lovers of money, also they understood all these words from
Him, but they mocked Jesus. He said to them;
you are just like who makes righteous in the sight
of God for yourselves before men, but God looks
at your hearts. For whoever, he exalts himself
more than among men is disgraceful in the sight
of God.

Jesus said the Law of God, and the prophets
were here to serve the people. God has used
them, and they brought the message of God to
His people. Until John arrived, God appointed
him to preach the Good News of the Kingdom
of God. Everyone was ready to draw near to the
Kingdom. Jesus said, even though if the heaven
and earth will disappear, but one little Law of
God will never fail or also will not pass away.

**"The law and the prophets were until John.
Since that time the kingdom of God has been
preached, and everyone is pressing into it. And
it is easier for heaven and earth to pass away
than for one tittle of the law to fail. "** Luke
16:14-17, NKJV.

Faith and Duty: They asked Him, Lord, 'increase our faith,' if you have faith as a small mustard seed, you may say to a big mountain to move out into the sea. You may commend the mulberry tree for pulling up the roots to be planted in the sea. Anything you would have to say, it shall obey your word. **"Death and life are in the power of the tongue"** Proverbs 18:21, NKJV. Because faith will come out of our hearts through our mouth.

Jesus gave a good story about a servant. He said, which of you have a servant who is looking after your sheep. He will speak to a servant when he has arrived in from the field, he would say, come in, and you may sit down to eat and rest? But I will cheerfully respond to him, make something for my lunch, and prepare it and give me what I wished for it! Does he acknowledge that servant, who is he?

Jesus said, your duty is serving anyone no matter who he is? It is our privilege to obey our Master to do what He said we would do. We are servants of God in a different area in the Body of Christ. We are ready to prepare any help or service for every man who will receive blessings of God.

"So the Lord said, "If you have faith as a mustard seed, you can say to this mulberry tree, 'Be pulled up by the roots and be planted in the sea,' and it would obey you." Luke 17:5-10, NKJV.

Unprofitable Servants: In this parable, we learn about the Master and the servants. Jesus appeared to declare our wonderful Father to us, that we accept all that Jesus accomplished for us on the cross. We look at ourselves as God truly cherished His children? But what are we receiving of these Words of Jesus? The Lord Jesus mentioned in these verses said: there are two servants, the unworthy servants, and the unprofitable servants? These two servants didn't put their faith to work.

We are chosen to become a child of God. We received an honor to be a servant. When we are living in the spirit of servanthood, we go through the challenge of life. We walk into a crisis, a temptation, and pride; then, we end up being an unprofitable servant?

An unprofitable servant, the one who was trying to complete a task and somehow he didn't make it. The result was that the servant goes on to look at other opportunities to perform the same purpose. Therefore, because of the failure in life to gave up to serve others. We need to establish faith, confidence, trust and hope to work as a servant in an enormous task.

"So likewise you, when you have done all those things which you are commanded, say, We are unprofitable servants. We have done what was our duty to do." Luke 17:7-10, NKJV.

Persistent Widow and a Judge: Persistent prayer is coming from the Word of God, and it reminds me of not to be a quitter in any circumcision, but being a person of victory. There was a widow in the town who desired to get help for her trouble. The widow was asking for mercy from a judge in the town. She was pleading for justice and crying for sympathy. She was expecting and waiting to receive a blessing. Because she was praying and seeking more, her mindset was not giving up, and she didn't quit but moved on!

The judge heard, and he said to himself, I don't believe God, either not care for any man. I will find a way to get rid of her. She is wearing me out. Finally, the judge gave her petition. The reason for prayer is not giving up. We must come to rest in God's presence into His peace and His joy in our lives.

Our Father in heaven chooses us to seek His face to experience Him better every day. Persistent prayer prepares us to become strong and courageous — our spiritual hunger desire to grow in His Word. Seeking Him by prayer, then we realized; why He gave Himself on the cross for our sins and sickness. Because He loves us, and He still loves us every day. Praying in spirit and reading His Words brings to a high level of maturity.

"yet because this widow troubles me I will avenge her, lest by her continual coming she weary me." Luke 18:1-8, NKJV.

Pharisee and Tax Collector: Here is an excellent parable that Jesus said about how a man can make himself a righteous person before God. Two men entered the temple to pray. One of the Pharisees was standing in the presence of God in the temple said: God, I am a perfect person; I thank you. I am not like other people who are standing beside me. I am not like a lawbreaker or thieves for money, unjustified, not committed adultery, or even I am not like this tax collector. I fast twice a week, what I earn, I will give my tithes.

And the other man was standing all the way back even he didn't look up to heaven. He was crying before God for mercy. He put his hands on his heart said: God, please have mercy on me; I am a sinner.

Jesus said: the Pharisee man went out of the temple with his righteousness, not receiving any forgiveness, he justified himself. But the other one who cried out to God for mercy and forgiveness of his sins, which God justified him. Jesus said: He who exalts himself shall be humbled, but the one who humbles himself shall be exalted before God.

"I tell you, this man went down to his house justified rather than the other; for everyone who exalts himself will be humbled, and he who humbles himself will be exalted." Luke 18:9-14, NKJV.

Jesus Comes to Zacchaeus' House: When Jesus arrived there and passed Jericho, the people were very excited to see Him. There was a short man named Zacchaeus. He couldn't see Jesus because of large crowded people in front of him. He decided to climb up a tree; it might be he will see Jesus by his own eyes. Zacchaeus saw Jesus while he was up a tree, now Jesus was walking, near to the tree. Jesus noticed there is a short man up a tree.

He knew his name and called him, said, Zacchaeus, you would come down, I must stay at your house today. Zacchaeus didn't know how to expect the honor that Jesus wanted to stay in his house. He was very excited; he came down from a tree; he went to Jesus. He received Him with great joy. The people were heard about it they complained about why Jesus will go to Zacchaeus's house. They said He is going to be a quest of sinners' home.

While Jesus was in the house with the people around Him, Zacchaeus touched by Jesus' presence in the house. God has revealed Himself to him, he said, Lord, look I give half of my goods to the poor, if I have taken anything unjustly from people by any false accusation, I will restore fourfold. Jesus was just amazed, He said, salvation has come to this place and in this house. Because Zacchaeus also came from the son of Abraham, and the Son of Man came to seek and save the lost man.

"And Jesus said to him, 'Today salvation has come to this house, because he also is a son of Abraham; for the Son of Man has come to seek

and to save that which was lost.'" Luke 19:1-10, NKJV.

Servants with Ten Minas: Jesus prepared another parable, and He was walking near Jerusalem, and people saw Him. They awaited the Kingdom of God will take place soon. He said: there was a nobleman who planned to leave a far country and to establish a kingdom for himself and coming back later. So, he wanted to choose ten servants to give them ten minas. They can do business with their minas and making more money by trading with a significant profit.

After a while, the nobleman came back; he called the ten servants that he trusted them. Those servants have received ten minas, and each servant had one mina. So, the first servant came to the nobleman; the servant said: master you gave me mina; I made it into trading business; I made an excellent profit with ten minas more. The nobleman said: you are a good servant, it will give you more responsibility for over ten cities.

The second servant came to him, and he said: master; I made a great profit to five minas. The master said: you are a very wise and faithful servant; you will be in charge of five cities. The next servant came to the nobleman told his master; I knew that you are a tough man. I was terrified. I couldn't make the mina into the trading business. Therefore, I hid it when you come back to give it back to you. The master saw him that his servant made a wrong decision, not having the courage to put mina into the business.

The nobleman said: You are a wicked man, according to your own words, I will judge you. Why did you have any faith to put your mina into bank business to make more interest profit? He said: Take his mina from him, give it to the one who has ten minas will know how to make more money.

It means; those who have more, it shall be given more and those who think they have it, but it will be taken away from them. And the nobleman said: those enemies came against me, they didn't want me to be king over them. He ordered all of them will be killed in front of a nobleman who became king over the land.

Meaning of parable: The nobleman is Jesus; he left the world and will come back as the King. Those servants represented as the followers of Jesus. The enemies of the King were the Jewish nation, and those have heard before. Everyone who listened to the Word of these days will reject King Jesus. He will defeat His enemies.

"For I say to you, that to everyone who has will be given; and from him who does not have, even what he has will be taken away from him. But bring here those enemies of mine, who did not want me to reign over them, and slay them before me." Luke 19:11-27, NKJV.

Jesus Triumphant Day: There was a triumphant day for Jesus' entry into Jerusalem. When Jesus reached near to Bethphage and Bethany, he came closer to the Mount of Olives. He ordered two of his disciples that they would go to the village. He told them when you go to the village you will find a donkey. You may lose him, and no one has ever ridden on it, is anyone asked you why do you untie the donkey. Tell them the Lord needs it.

Then his disciples went to the village; they saw precisely where the donkey was, and the owner of the donkey asked them. At the same word, Jesus spoke to His two disciples before the event happened; they were amazed. So, these two disciples brought the donkey to Jesus. He sat on as they went toward the Mount of Olives. The multitudes of people, along with His disciples.

They started to rejoice and praise the God of Israel with a loud voice. Saying**: "Blessed is the King who comes in the name of the Lord! Peace in heaven and glory in the highest!"**

Some lawmakers and the Pharisees saw these people who were walking behind Jesus, which he was riding on the donkey. They were rejoicing with the shout of praise to God. They said to Jesus: Teacher, you may rebuke your disciples. We don't need to listen to all their shouting. Jesus answered: if they would stop rejoicing in God, the stone will begin to cry out.

"But He answered and said to them, I tell you that if these should keep silent, the stones would immediately cry out." Luke 19:28-40, NKJV.

Paying Taxes to Caesar or Not: When Jesus taught people about the Good News of the Kingdom of God. Those leaders tried to catch Him to deliver Jesus to the authority of the governor. They sent some of their followers to hear Him when He taught the Word of God. Maybe they will find something happened will come against Him. They were all standing listing to Him.

They asked Him: Teacher! Is it right to pay taxes to Ceaser or not? Jesus looked at them, give me a denarius. He asked them: whose picture on the denarius? They said: It is Caesar's. Therefore, pay your taxes to Ceaser's, and the other side is God's, and it belonged to God's. They were all wondered how He answered with the wisdom of God. They couldn't ask Him any question. They kept silent.

"And He said to them, Render therefore to Caesar the things that are Caesar's, and to God the things that are God's." Luke 20:20-26, NKJV.

CHAPTER FIVE

Parables in the Book of John

The New Birth: There was a man of the Pharisees named, Nicodemus who had an enormously influential in his position as the ruler of the Jews. He came to Jesus at night; he wanted to learn new things from Jesus. He asked Him, Rabbi; We have seen you, how you teach a Word of God. We know your Word is from God; we see all signs you do unless God is with You. He asked again, How can a man is very old, is it possible a man goes back to his mother's womb, be born again?

Jesus answered, unless a man is born again, he cannot be able to enter the Kingdom of God.

When a man is born of the flash, is flash, which a man is born of the spirit, is spirit. Do not be surprised. I say to you; you shall be born of water and the spirit. Jesus told another example: if the wind blows where it wants to blow! But you hear only the sound of it. You cannot see by your own physical eyes or don't know where the winds come from or where it goes? Everyone needs to be born of the spirit.

Then Nicodemus asked another question saying, 'How can these things happen?' Jesus answered, you teach, and you are the teacher of Israel, you don't know about these things? What we have seen and what we testify in the spirit. If I told you the earthly matter of this life about the One who is the Son of Man came down from heaven. Jesus is saying if we are living in spirit, we understand the things of the spirit. If we are thinking and living in the earthly things, is the flash, we can understand the fleshly mind only.

Jesus continued saying, whoever believes in the Son of Man shall not perish. **"For God so loved the world that He gave His only begotten Son, that whoever believes in Him should not perish but have everlasting life."** John 3:16, NKJV. He preached to Nicodemus said, God has not sent His Son to condemn the world, but the world should be saved through the Son of God. Jesus is proclaiming, "He who believes in Him, shall not be condemned, he who has not believed in Him has already condemned himself." Because of our faith and believing in the Son of God, Jesus will save our lost souls. And our new spirit would have everlasting life in heaven with Him.

Jesus declared that the Light of Him has come; man loves darkness rather than light because man's deeds are evil. If everyone who goes after evil, engaging the things of darkness would hate the Light. If you come to the Light, your deeds shall be lest exposed. He who loves the truth will accept a new Life, and a new Light shall shine on him.

"For everyone practicing evil hates the light and does not come to the light, lest his deeds should be exposed. But he who does the truth comes to the light, that his deeds may be clearly seen, that they have been done in God." John 3:1-21, NKJV.

Honor the Father and the Son: The reason the Jews wanted to persecute Jesus, He had done many good things on the Sabbath. They sought to accuse Him and to kill Him, but Jesus said, My Father has done marvelous work, and I have been working the Will of My Father. At the same time, they wanted to kill Him because Jesus made Himself equal with God. They thought no one could make himself equal with God. Jesus made a clear statement here said, the Son cannot do anything by His own and cannot do without the work of the Father. The Father does the work, and the Son will do as well.

The Father loves His son, showed Him all things to fulfill the plan to bring Salvation to the world. He teaches many things through His Son that it may astonish you in your own eyes. If the Father raises the dead to life, the Son also does the same. The father will judge no one, but He had given all judgment to the Son. You must honor the Son as you honor God as the Father. Those who do not accept the Son does not honor the Father who sent His only begotten Son who died and rose again.

"For the Father judges no one, but has committed all judgment to the Son, that all should honor the Son just as they honor the Father. He who does not honor the Son does not honor the Father who sent Him." John 5:16-23, NKJV.

Jesus the Light of the World: There was a very early morning, Jesus came back from the

Mount of Olives. He went into the temple, and many people came along with Him. They sat down, and He taught them the Word of God. They were all hungry for hearing Him. Suddenly these lawmakers, the scribes, and Pharisees came, and they brought a woman, and they put her in the midst. People were there and watching what is happening here?

They said to Jesus, Teacher, what would you say about this woman who was caught in adultery! In Moses's law, had commanded us when a woman caught in this such act, it should be stoned? So, what do you say about this? In fact, they wanted to test Jesus about this situation to find something to accuse Him. Jesus sat and stooped down to write on the ground with his fingers, even though He heard from them, but it may seem, He heard nothing! But they kept asking Him the questions.

Finally, He said to them, is anyone who is among you without sin, you may throw a stone at her first. Jesus stooped down one more time, and he wrote on the ground again. At the same time, those people heard what Jesus said to them, and there was conviction in their hearts by the conscience spirit. They went out one by one left the place. No one stood there, and they have gone on their way. Jesus was alone, and the woman was still sitting in the midst by herself.

Jesus saw there is no one except Him and the woman alone. He called the woman, where are those accusers of yours? The woman answered, Lord, no one left here. There were gone. Jesus replied, I will not condemn you either; you may go home, give not yourself to sin again. I am the Light of the World. He who follows Me would receive the Light, and he will not walk in darkness. But he can have a new life with Glorious majestic the Light of Jesus forever.

"Then Jesus spoke to them again, saying, "I am the light of the world. He who follows Me shall not walk in darkness, but have the light of life." John 8:1-12, NKJV.

Jesus Defends His Self-Witness: While Jesus was teaching the people in the temple, those Pharisees came to Him, said, You make a witness of Yourself; if you do, but Your witness is not true. Jesus answered, because I make a witness of Myself, I know my witness is true. I know, I came from My Father, even though I speak the truth to you, you still do not believe it. You would judge according to the flesh, He said, I will judge no one. Again, I do judge, and My judgment is true, for My Father is with Me, He who sent me.

My Father is my witness. Also, it is written in the Law that it will establish the testimonies of two are true. I testify of the One who is with Me, and I bear witness of Myself. They asked Him; we want to know about your Father? Where is He? Jesus said you don't want to know Me or neither nor My Father. If you know Me who I AM. You will know My Father as well. They have not touched or laid hands on Him because His time has not come yet.

Our witness is the Word of God, which is confirming to us by the Holy Spirit. We witness the Good News of Jesus will bring a new revelation, which is hearing the Word. Only the Holy Spirit would have to reveal Jesus to everyone who wants to listen to the Word and to confess Jesus as the Son of God. And the Holy Spirit is stirring the heart of any man who is hearing the Salvation of God.

The Spirit of God is revealing about sin in the heart for a confession by repentance. And then we believe forgiveness; we will receive it by His Grace. If you have not recognized your sin and you would have to confess it now. He is able to forgive all your sins and give you a new life and change your destiny.

"Jesus answered, "You know neither Me nor My Father. If you had known Me, you would have known My Father also." These words Jesus spoke in the treasury, as He taught in the temple; and no one laid hands on Him, for His hour had not yet come." John 8:13-20, NKJV.

The Truth Shall Make You Free: Jesus taught and preached the Word by the power of God to those who believed in Him. He said, if you dwell in My Word, you will be My disciples. Then you shall know the truth, and the truth makes you free. Those Jews were there and listing to Him, asking Him, do you realize we are Abraham's descendants; we have never been in bondage, how would you say that the truth will make us free.

Jesus said you had committed sins; you are a slave to sin, and your sins will destroy your life. A slave who is living in sin, it cannot live forever, but the Son of God lives forever. Jesus said, Now you are living in sin, the Son is here, and He came to set you free. Jesus declared that He is the Way, the Truth, and the Life.

Let's repent our sins, and He is able to set us free from our unrighteousness, and our guilt of life. We need freedom, and the joy and blessings of God would come by His Grace.

"Jesus answered them, Most assuredly, I say to you, whoever commits sin is a slave of sin. And a slave does not abide in the house forever, but a son abides forever. Therefore if the Son makes you free, you shall be free indeed." John 8:31-36, NKJV.

Jesus the True Shepherd: Jesus was preaching about the true shepherd. He said, he who does not enter through the shelter's sheep door, it can not be able to enter in other entries. He who will allow the sheep will enter through the door gate is the Shepherd. Those who will come to enter the Kingdom of God through the door, they must hear the voice of the Shepherd. But those thieves and robbers are trying to climb up some other way to enter by the door.

Those sheep belong to the shepherd, and they can recognize Him. He will lead His own sheep to come in. But those who do not belong to Him, they cannot recognize His voice, and they will not be able to enter. Sheep cannot follow the voice of strangers, and they will only follow the sound of the shepherd. The shepherd will lead

His sheep into a place of protection, security, and provisions.

"But he who enters by the door is the shepherd of the sheep. To him the doorkeeper opens, and the sheep hear his voice; and he calls his own sheep by name and leads them out." John 10:1-6, NKJV.

Jesus the Good Shepherd: Jesus said I am the good shepherd. I will watch over my sheep, and I am the door of every sheep will enter through the door of shelter sheep's door. If anyone enters through the door, it will come in and go out will find good pasture. The thief had a plan to come to steal, to kill, and to destroy everyone. But I came to give life, and they may have life abundantly. I am the door, and if anyone wants to enter, he shall be saved.

I know my own sheep, My Father will know Me, I lay down My life for My sheep. I have other sheep; also, they will hear My voice, and I will bring them with one flock and one shepherd together. My Father knows me, and He loves me. I can lie down my life for sheep, and I have the power to take it back again. My Father gave me this command.

After these things, Jesus preached to the Jews. It became a conflict among the Jews. They gathered together and said; we don't need to listen to Him, and we think He has a demon. Then others said, We believe the Words He preached; the devil does not speak as He does. Can a demon heal or open the blind eyes? Jesus heals, and He is the Healer.

"I am the good shepherd. The good shepherd gives His life for the sheep." John 10:7-21, NKJV.

The Shepherd Knows His Sheep: It was winter and the feast of dedication in Jerusalem. Jesus came to the temple in Solomon's porch. The Jews surrounded Him, and they asked a question; how long do you keep us in uncertainty? Are you the Christ, tell us the truth. Jesus answered, I said before, but you do not believe it. I carry the plan of My Father, everything I do in my Father's name will have a witness of Me. You still do not believe it, because you are not one of My sheep.

Jesus said, My sheep can hear my voice; they obey Me and follow Me. I will lead them to eternal life, and they will not perish. No one would take my sheep away from out of my hands. My

Father has given them to Me. My Father and I are one.

"My Father, who has given them to Me, is greater than all; and no one is able to snatch them out of My Father's hand. I and My Father are one." John 10:22-30, NKJV.

The Triumphal Entry: On the day of the arrival of Jesus to Jerusalem, many people came to the feast. They heard that Jesus is coming this way; the people wanted to meet Him with great joy; They gathered branches of palm trees. They went out to see Him. They cheered with a powerful voice saying:

"Hosanna! 'Blessed is He who comes in the name of the Lord!'

The King of Israel!" John 12:13

They found a young donkey then He sat on it, as it is written:

"Fear not, daughter of Zion;

Behold, your King is coming, Sitting on a donkey's colt." John 12:15

The people rejoiced and were happy that the sweet presence of Jesus was among them. His disciples couldn't understand at first. But Jesus was glorified there, and they had to remember these things were written about Jesus. He performed healing and miracles. He raised Lazarus from death to life. His disciples were there as a witness in the time of Jesus's wonders in front of many people. The reason was the people came to meet Him, to thank Him, what He has done for all the people in many cities. The Pharisees saw the event saying, the whole world has gone after Jesus.

"For this reason the people also met Him, because they heard that He had done this sign. The Pharisees therefore said among themselves, "You see that you are accomplishing nothing. Look, the world has gone after Him!" John 12:12-19, NKJV.

Who Has Believed Our Report?: Jesus had many signs and wonders before Jews' eyes, but they still did not believe in Him. As we read, the Word said that Isaiah has prophesied that he saw Jesus's Glory in heaven then spoken of Him.

Isaiah prophesied that Jesus would enter the world as a human in the flesh. He would accomplish the Father's plan and how He would give His life for the sin of the world. He would die and rose again. Isaiah declares that Jesus would come as the Messiah. We must believe the Word by Isaiah spoke, and he proclaimed that God

would deliver such the Messiah to us. They asked
many questions; they had a doubt and could not
understand how the word of Isaiah has fulfilled
already, he spoke:

"Lord, who has believed our report?

**And to whom has the arm of the Lord been
revealed?"**

Therefore they could not believe, because Isaiah said again:

**"He has blinded their eyes and hardened
their hearts,**

Lest they should see with their eyes,

**Lest they should understand with their
hearts and turn,**

So that I should heal them." John 12:37-41,
NKJV.

Walk in the Light: Many lawmakers heard
about Jesus's preaching; they believed in Him.
But the Pharisees listened to the Word of God
from Jesus, and they didn't confess in Him. Jesus
mentioned, these Pharisees would like to have
praise of men, more than to praise God.

Jesus said if he wants to believe in Me, but it
must also believe the One who sent Me. If anyone wants to see me, they would have to see
the One who sent Me. I came as a light into the

world. Anyone who believes in Me, they should not dwell in darkness. If anyone who does not believe in Me; I did not come to judge. But I came to bring salvation into the world.

Is anyone who rejects Me, and does not want to receive My words, it will be judged according to his last day. I did not speak on My own authority, but My Father who sent Me. He gave Me a command of what to speak. It is His command for having everlasting life. Whatever I would speak, My Father has given Me to speak.

"For I have not spoken on My own authority; but the Father who sent Me gave Me a command, what I should say and what I should speak. And I know that His command is everlasting life. Therefore, whatever I speak, just as the Father has told Me, so I speak." John 12:42-50, NKJV.

The New Commandment: The Lord Jesus made a great statement about having a new commandment. He said the Son of Man would be glorified, and God is glorified in Him as well. As we know, God is glorified in Jesus. He predicted about Himself. He said, 'My children, I will be with you for a short while.' Jesus said you would seek Me. He told the Jews about where I am going, but you cannot come.

Now I will give a new commandment, and I have loved you, you must love one another. If you love one another, and they would have to know that you are My true disciples.

"A new commandment I give to you, that you love one another; as I have loved you, that you also love one another. By this all will know that you are My disciples, if you have love for one another." John 13:31-35, NKJV.

The Way, the Truth, and the Life: Jesus encouraged us not to let our hearts be troubled. He said if anyone who believes in God, you would also believe in Me. There will be many mansions in My Father's house; I will go to arrange a home for you. I will be coming back again and take you to Myself; that where I am, there you would also be with Me. He taught to His disciples, one of the disciples, Thomas, asked Him, Lord, we want to know where you are going, and we don't know the way?

He is the authority and the law of truth. He is the One who has established: The Way, The Truth and The Way in Scriptures. As we experience, Jesus is the Truth; we just trust in Him in our hearts. Instead, we believe an eternal truth. He is absolutely trustworthy, and because of this reason, we can entrust every word of God. Jesus declares that God revealed Himself to His servants and us.

"Jesus said to him, 'I am the way, the truth, and the life. No one comes to the Father except through Me.'" John 14:1-6, NKJV.

The Answered Prayer: Jesus assured us about the prayer, is anyone who believes in Me, what I do, and he can also do in My name. You may do the great works that I did, and you can do when I go to My Father. Is anyone who believes in My Word, and whatever you ask anything in My name, I will do it. May My Father in heaven shall be glorified in the Son.

When we pray, we ask Him for His presence to be released by His Holy Spirit. He will confirm His Words to us, and we call upon His name, the name of Jesus shall be exalted forever. He answers all our prayers because His Words are truth, and His Words are full of the spirit of Living God. Today we can ask Him anything in His name. He will hear us, and He can do powerful miracles in the mighty name of Jesus. Amen.

"And whatever you ask in My name, that I will do, that the Father may be glorified in the Son. If you ask anything in My name, I will do it." John 14:12-14, NKJV.

Jesus Promises Another Helper: Jesus had given a true promise that when he ascended to heaven. The father sent another helper, which is the Holy Spirit. Jesus said, you truly love Me; you must keep My commandments. As we believe the Holy Spirit is here with us, He lives in us. And the Lord Jesus gave the Holy Spirit to teach, to lead, to guide, to comfort us in our lives, also to dwell in the church. As we experience, the Holy Spirit is the spirit of the truth and is revealing Jesus to the church.

When we believe in the Son of God, the Holy Spirit is revealing Jesus as our Lord and Savior to everyone who has faith. Jesus said, when you know Me, you know My truth; it is an excellent work of the Spirit of God. He is with us until Jesus would come back to earth again. Let's rejoice in His goodness.

"the Spirit of truth, whom the world cannot receive, because it neither sees Him nor knows Him; but you know Him, for He dwells with you

and will be in you. I will not leave you orphans; I will come to you." John 14:15-18, NKJV.

The Gift of His Peace: The Lord Jesus has spoken to us about His peace. The Holy Spirit is teaching us to all truth. Jesus said: He would bring all good remembrance to us what He said in His Words. The Lord Jesus told us: I would leave My peace with you. The world cannot give peace as I provide you with peace. Do not have trouble in this world, or do not be afraid. Do not allow your heart to become cold in life and to grow into fear. If you love me, you may rejoice in Me, to walk in the truth and peace.

Living in peace is a gift of God; we will have no trouble in this world when we come to Jesus and accept Him. We receive His salvation by faith, and His peace is like flowing water in us. We grow in a new spiritual life. Therefore we learn how to live in peace in ourselves and with others. Because our spirit has changed to a new spirit from God, who gave us a free gift of salvation.

"Peace I leave with you, My peace I give to you; not as the world gives do I give to you. Let not your heart be troubled, neither let it be afraid." John 14:25-31, NKJV.

The True Vine: Jesus was preaching about Himself that He is the true vine, and He mentioned that His Father is also the Vinedresser. Jesus taught about every disciple who lives in Him; it cannot bear fruit; the father takes away. If every disciple would bear fruit, the Father flourishes that may bring more fruits. The Lord Jesus spoke of His true disciples that they heard the Word because Jesus preached the Word.

They received cleanness of spirit. When they listened to the Word, the presence of Jesus, which is the Word, has sanctified them. He said if you dwell in Me, and I dwell in you as well. My followers cannot bear fruits by themselves unless they have to reside in the vine, which is Me.

Jesus spoke here; If you do not reside in Me, without Me, you can do nothing. If you cannot bear fruits, they will cast out all dried branches into the fire; they will be burned. If you ask yourself, what is your desire, and if you ask Him. Jesus said it should be done to you, and My Father shall be glorified. If you bear fruits, then they will know that you are My disciples.

"If you abide in Me, and My words abide in you, you will ask what you desire, and it shall be done for you. By this My Father is glorified,

that you bear much fruit; so you will be My disciples." John 15:1-8, NKJV.

The World's Hatred: Jesus will tell us that
the world hates us because of our faith in Him.
The world hates Him before they hate us, as the
world would have their own love for themselves.
He said I had chosen you out of this world. They
hate you. He reminds us, a servant called to serve
and had decided to serve others. He is not greater than His Master. The world tried to persecute
Me, and they will persecute you as well.

They will not allow you to have your faith in
Him and to keep you not to preach the Word.
They will do all these things to hurt you in My
name' sake because they do not know the Father
who sent Me into this world. I came to speak
about the world's sin, and they may listen and
receive the Father's forgiveness. If they hate Me,
they hate the Father as well. It might fulfill it,
which is written in the law that they hate for no
reason.

"If I had not done among them the works
which no one else did, they would have no sin;
but now they have seen and also hated both Me
and My Father. But this happened that the word
might be fulfilled which is written in their law,

'They hated Me without a cause.'" John 15:18-25, NKJV.

The Work of the Holy Spirit: Let's ask ourselves, what is the work of the Holy Spirit? Jesus said, if I go away, maybe none of you would ask Me; where are You going? I may say about My leaving, which will fill your heart with sorrow. I tell the truth that it might be right for you that I go away. The Helper is the Holy Spirit will not come to you until I go away from here. The Holy Spirit will reveal a conviction of sin, righteousness, and judgment in the world because the world will not believe in Me. I go to My Father, you will see Me no more.

The Helper will convict the world about judgment; the ruler of this world will be judged. Jesus mentioned to His disciples that He had many things to say, but they cannot bear them now. But when the spirit of truth would come, He leads, guides you into all truth. He will tell you whatever He hears from Me. He will say to you. The Holy Spirit will reveal everything that whatever the Father has are Mine. He will declare to you with the truth.

"He will glorify Me, for He will take of what is Mine and declare it to you. All things that the

Father has are Mine. Therefore I said that He [c]will take of Mine and declare it to you." John 16:5-15, NKJV.

Jesus Warns and Comforts His Disciples: Jesus has already warned us not to stumble and to become strong in Him. He said if they force you out of houses of worship, or they are trying to kill you, they think killing is one of their offering service to God. They will continue doing this kind of act to you because they would not know My Father nor Me. These things are going to happen, which I told you before, but I am with you.

"But these things I have told you, that when the time comes, you may remember that I told you of them. And these things I did not say to you at the beginning, because I was with you." John 16:1-4, NKJV.

Sorrow Will Turn to Joy: Jesus has shared about our sorrow turned into joy. He was saying to His disciples that He will be leaving, not to see Him for a little while, but to see Him again. He goes to the Father. His disciples say, what is He talking about? Why He is speaking, not see Him for a little while. Jesus realized His disciples had a desire to know about where their Master is going? He knew that His disciples thought they would go through sorrow and with grieve. Jesus said If your life goes in troubles and regret. The world will make you sorrowful and but you rejoice over your problems. Jesus said, but you remember, your sorrow will be turned into joy.

Jesus gave a good sample: He said, a pregnant woman should be ready for going to labor and giving birth to a baby. But during her child labor, she will have pain until she delivers a baby. After giving birth, she will not remember her labor experience any longer. Because she would have great joy with a child as she will not even remember her pain in labor hours.

The Lord Jesus encouraged us to pray and ask the Father in His name, if we ask anything in His name, we shall receive it. We may have the fullness of joy in the Lord.

"And in that day you will ask Me nothing. Most assuredly, I say to you, whatever you ask the Father in My name He will give you. Until now you have asked nothing in My name. Ask, and you will receive, that your joy may be full." John 16:16-24, NKJV.

Jesus Has Overcome the World: Jesus came to overcome the world for bringing a new life to everyone who will receive a great destiny. He said these words I have told you in expressive language, but the time is taking place when I will not talk to you in expressive language. But I will say to you clearly about the Father. In the day comes, you will call on My name. I do not tell you now, but I shall pray for you to the Father.

The Father Himself cares for you because you have shown your love to Me. You have believed in Me that I came from God. I have come into the world and going back to the Father. His disciples said, look at how you are speaking clearly. We currently know that there is no need that anyone would ask any questions of you. We believe that God sent you here for us.

Jesus answered: you believe in Me now, the time comes that you will be scattered and going back to your life again. You all leave me alone, but I know I am not alone because the Father is with Me. Jesus spoke of the future what will be? He encouraged His disciples, and you may live in peace when He has gone back to the Father. Jesus warned us to be with Him all of our lives.

Jesus predicted that His followers would have persecution and tribulation in the world. At the same time, He said, rejoice in Me. Jesus brought peace and overcome the world.

"Jesus answered them, "Do you now believe? Indeed the hour is coming, yes, has now come, that you will be scattered, each to his own, and will leave Me alone. And yet I am not alone, because the Father is with Me. These things I have spoken to you, that in Me you may have peace. In the world you will have tribulation; but be of good cheer, I have overcome the world." John 16:25-33, NKJV.

CHAPTER SIX

How to become a Christian?

A Christian who is a follower of Jesus and trusts in him. The Bible gives a simple explanation so we can have a relationship with Him. We will have a spiritual experience as we become a born-again Christian believer. The great news of the Christian doctrine appears with the concept that God has chosen us. He who formed us and created us in the image of His Son on this earth. I want just to take this opportunity to share about how we can have a personal relationship with Jesus by faith. It is essential to follow the way of God's Word is better than doing any other ritual Christianity. It will not help us to become a Christian believer.

When we recognize that we have sinned against God, and our sin will separate us from God, and it will lead us to death. We cannot make ourselves clean or forgive our own sins. Jesus came to be born and to die on the cross for our sinfulness, wickedness, iniquity, and immorality; he sacrificed his life for our good. He shed His blood for our sickness. Now we can go to Him by faith with no condemnation and no judgment.

Becoming a Christian is to have a simple faith in the Lord, learning His Word, allowing ourselves to have a fellowship with other Christians believers in the church. Then we build up our confidence in the Word and living more in the peace of Christ. We grow into a better spiritual maturity in walking with the Lord. When we move forward in faith, we develop our confidence in the Word of God only.

Let's focus on this part that we "believe" that Jesus is the Son of God. We are the sinners; we all need a Savior. He can save us from our sins. Now we repent our sins and accept Jesus into our hearts. It is very simple to believe Jesus by faith. I will describe the few steps to remind us to make peace with our Heavenly Father, who loves us.

1. Believing in One true God and His Word
2. Repenting your sins
3. Inviting Jesus to come into your heart
4. Receiving Jesus as your Savior and Lord
5. To get baptized in water
6. Finding a Christian Fellowship to attend
7. Growing in the Spiritual life every day

When you follow these simple steps, you become a born-again Christian believer and welcome into God's family. When you are devoting your time in His presence and studying the Word of God, then the Holy Spirit reveals Jesus to you. I am thrilled that you make the right decision to accept Jesus as your Savior. According to the Bible, you are saved, and He will forgive all your sins and wipe out your tears and restore you from all your iniquity. Then, remember your name is written in the Book of Life in heaven. I want to lead you a short prayer of salvation.

Repeat after me:

Heavenly Father, I thank you for your Son Jesus; you sent Him to die on the cross for me in my place. He rose, and He is alive again. I repent from all my sins; I invite Jesus to come into my heart; I believe Jesus as my Lord and my Savior.

Thank you for caring for me and accepting me as a child of God. In Jesus' name. Amen.

Conclusion

I will conclude this book by giving me the honor to serve you with many greatest parables in the Bible. In this book, we will learn so many beautiful stories that Jesus taught His disciples and to followers with spiritual messages. May we all apply the Word of God in our own personal walk with the Lord Jesus? I am thrilled that I had this opportunity to go through, and to summarize each parable to make an uplifting message with the magnificent God. We will find out that God can speak to us through many different stories. It was a joy to present a demonstration of the power of God.

The parables of Jesus told with many records in the first three Gospels. In the Gospel of John, we cannot find any parable at all. But we discover excellent teaching with the illustrations, so-called, the good shepherd with love the Father. Jesus' parables illustrate many aspects of the kingdom of God. God has manifested His love and salvation through these powerful parables and stories to bring us back to Himself.

We all have a desire going after a new life with the truth. It would have to come with our repentance and to trust in Him. He loves to see we are obedient to His Word. These stories and illustrations of Jesus to give a good revelation who we are in Christ? Jesus made straightforward stories and a short parable for our understanding. It may these parables would have an impact on the mind, to become an interest in our hearts. That's why Jesus made it easy to accept salvation.

He prepared the Kingdom of God for us that we can experience His Way. No one can receive the salvation of God without hearing the Word. As we understand, reading and hearing the Word would create faith. These parables would make an enormous conviction for any man who wants to know Jesus. We must remember that the Word of God is building up our faith, our trust, and our hope, then we believe Jesus as our Lord and Savior.

This book will help you, excite you, and strengthen you to grow into a mighty man or woman of God. Sharing incredible stories about the Kingdom of God can inspire us to stay focus and effective in this life. May this book serve you and revive you to build up your faith in the Lord. I dream that this book will reach millions of Christian believers around the world. Thank you for supporting me, and it was my privilege to serve you through this book, and may God bless you.

In the end, I would like to present my other books to you:

- **Manifestation of Prayer**
- **Encouraging Stories in the Bible**
- **Authority in the Bible**
- **Healing Miracles of Jesus**

About the Author

D r. Daniel Kazemian has dedicated his life to the nonprofit organization International Evangelistic Ministry, to preach the Good News by the anointing of the Holy Spirit. In June 1993, he was ordained to the ministry in the National Church of God by Dr. T. L. Lowery in Washington, DC. He has since become one of today's most dynamic charismatic preachers. Christ walked into his life in January 1985, and Daniel was transformed into an exciting, enthusiastic dynamo for God. He's passionate about sharing God's love and saving grace with everyone, as well as healing the sick. Daniel started his evangelistic career and his radio/TV ministry in Denmark-Scandinavia and abroad. He is now serving in the prophetic and healing ministry, and he ministers in churches, seminars, conventions, crusades, and anywhere the Spirit of God leads him.

Daniel earned his associate degree from the National Bible College and Seminary in June 1993 in Fort Washington, Maryland, and a bachelor's degree, a master's degree, and a Doctor of Theology degree from the International Theological Seminary in July 1996 in Plymouth, Florida. He is the president of the nonprofit organization, International Evangelistic Ministry, located in Gainesville, Georgia.

Contact him through email:
ieministry@hotmail.com

Visit our website:
www.InternationalEvangelisticMinistry.com